MASTERWORKS IN WOOD: CHINA AND JAPAN

DONALD JENKINS
with the assistance of
Robin Scribnick

PORTLAND ART MUSEUM
November 4 through December 5, 1976

ASIA HOUSE GALLERY
January 13 through March 20, 1977

*This project is supported by a grant from the
National Endowment for the Arts in Washington, D.C.,
a Federal agency, and by a grant from the
American Revolution Bicentennial Commission of Oregon*

Portland Art Museum
Portland, Oregon

LENDERS TO THE EXHIBITION

Mr. and Mrs. James Alsdorf
Winnetka, Illinois

Art Institute of Chicago
Chicago, Illinois

The Art Museum, Princeton University
Princeton, New Jersey

Asian Art Museum of San Francisco
San Francisco, California

The Brooklyn Museum
Brooklyn, New York

The Mary and Jackson Burke Foundation
New York, New York

Cleveland Museum of Art
Cleveland, Ohio

Mrs. Usher P. Coolidge
Ipswich, Massachusetts

The Denver Art Museum
Denver, Colorado

Mr. and Mrs. Myron Falk, Jr.
New York, New York

N. V. Hammer
New York, New York

Honolulu Academy of Arts
Honolulu, Hawaii

Kimbell Art Museum
Fort Worth, Texas

The Metropolitan Museum of Art
New York, New York

Minneapolis Museum of Arts
Minneapolis, Minnesota

Museum of Fine Arts
Boston, Massachusetts

William Rockhill Nelson Gallery of Art-
Atkins Museum of Fine Arts
Kansas City, Missouri

Langdon J. Plumer
Exeter, New Hampshire

Portland Art Museum
Portland, Oregon

Mr. and Mrs. John D. Rockefeller III
New York, New York

The St. Louis Art Museum
St. Louis, Missouri

Seattle Art Museum
Seattle, Washington

The University of Michigan Museum of Art
Ann Arbor, Michigan

William Watson
London, England

Two anonymous lenders

The theme of this exhibition is an ambitious one. I have attempted to view as a totality a tradition that is usually seen only piecemeal: the tradition of Far Eastern wood sculpture. In doing so, I have relied on Western collections exclusively, fully aware that the greatest monuments of that tradition are still to be found in Japan. Yet no apology need be made for the works included here. Their quality is uniformly high; and if they provide only an incomplete view of the rich tradition they have been asked to represent, the fault is not theirs.

The lenders to this exhibition have been asked to part with precious objects, many of great fragility, for upwards of half a year. That they have consented to do so is a testimony to their generosity. Many of them extended themselves to provide me with specific information regarding details of structure and condition. I am grateful to them all.

I would also like to give special thanks to Robin Scribnick, Exhibition Research Assistant, and Holly Magowan, Museum Apprentice during 1975-76, who helped me with research; to Bette Holman, my Executive Secretary, who bore much of the brunt of this project; to Robert Peirce, Museum Editor, who reviewed the entire text; and to Charles Politz, whose superb sense of design is apparent throughout the catalogue. Michael Cunningham provided valuable assistance in tracking down reference works in Japan.

This exhibition is the fifth and last of a series of five Masterworks in Wood exhibitions organized as a Bicentennial project of the Portland Art Museum. The series was made possible by grants from the National Endowment for the Arts, the Oregon Bicentennial Commission, and numerous private and corporate donors. I am indebted to Asia House Gallery and its Director, Allen Wardwell, for their assistance in this project and for making it possible for the exhibition to be seen in New York.

Donald Jenkins

TABLE OF CONTENTS

For the ancient Chinese, wood was one of the five elements along with earth, metal, fire, and water, and over the centuries it has continued to hold a very special place both in China and Japan. The great monuments of European architecture are almost all of stone, but the villas, palaces, and temples of the Far East are principally of wood. (In fact, one word for architecture in Chinese is *t'u-mu*, "earth and wood.") In Japan, the use of wood has been particularly extensive, touching almost every aspect of daily life; chopsticks, clogs, soupbowls, bathtubs, and combs are only a few of the articles traditionally made of this material. It is very likely that the Chinese once relied on wood to a similar extent, only turning to substitute materials after their forests were used up.

As one might expect in light of their long association with the material, the people of the Far East are unusually sensitive to the special characteristics of different kinds of wood, admiring some for their lightness and workability, others for their strength or the beauty of their grain, yet others for their fragrance. This sensitivity to wood, this appreciation of its special properties, is particularly apparent in Far Eastern wood sculpture; in fact, probably no other sculptural tradition is its equal in this respect. No wonder, then, that Japanese sculptors have always preferred wood over other materials and Chinese sculptors have held it in almost equal esteem. There have been periods when wood was paramount in Western sculpture, but in the Far East, or at least in Japan, it has always been paramount. In a very real sense, therefore, this exhibition can be said to explore the mainstream of Far Eastern sculpture.

So sweeping a statement obviously requires qualification. The bulk of Chinese sculpture in this country, at least that portion of it dated prior to the Sung Dynasty, is of stone or bronze. One could easily come away with the impression that wood played only a very minor role in early Chinese sculpture. This is true, however, only so far as *surviving* sculpture is concerned. Wood is a notoriously perishable material, and wooden images were particularly vulnerable to the natural and man-caused disasters—fires, floods, earthquakes, invasions—that have ravaged China over the centuries. Periodic persecutions of Buddhism must have taken an additional toll, and even simple neglect must have accounted for the loss of others. As a result, it is difficult to gain a sense of the extent to which wood actually was used for sculpture in China. It is very likely, in fact, that its popularity varied from period to period. It may well be that clay, bronze, and dry lacquer were used in preference to wood during the seventh and eighth centuries. At least we know this to be true of Japanese sculpture which was under heavy Chinese influence at that time. Even so, there can be no doubt that wood sculpture was produced in quantity in China prior to the Sung Dynasty; the relatively small number of surviving examples is highly misleading.

One can gain a better sense of the extent to which wood was used in Japan. Though fires, storms, and earthquakes exacted a toll there too, the country was never invaded, and it suffered much less political turmoil. The hold of tradition was strong; Buddhism was never persecuted; and treasured images have been preserved intact for centuries in the storehouses and Golden Halls of the principal temples.

It should be pointed out, however, that much of the wood sculpture that has survived otherwise has done so only in fragmentary condition. Even where the images themselves have survived without damage—and many of them have not—they are apt to be missing some attribute or ornament originally deemed essential. Moreover, Buddhist sculpture, in particular, was designed to be part of a total setting which could not help but add to its effectiveness. It must be remembered that these images were either icons—i.e., objects of veneration—and as such would have been elevated or enthroned above the worshipper, or were attendants or guardians of these principal images. All of these, icons and attendants alike, would be arrayed on a platform or altar symbolizing Mt. Sumeru, the mythical peak at the center of the Buddhist universe. The principal images, upraised on lotus pedestals (see No. 28), would be backed by gleaming mandorlas, or halos, and a richly carved canopy would hang overhead. Invariably the four heavenly kings would stand guard at each of the four corners of the altar. If the central image was a Buddha, it would probably be flanked by at least two bodhisattvas. If the Buddha was Amida Nyorai, images of bodhisattvas and heavenly musicians might be affixed to its halo or even the wall behind. Sometimes veritable troops of figures were arrayed across the altar. In the Sanjūsangen-dō in Kyoto, one thousand images of the Thousand-armed Kannon, five hundred to a side, flank a large central image of the same deity.

There is at least one other important respect in which we no longer see many of these sculptures in the way that they were intended to be seen. Many of them—in fact nearly all the Buddhist images—were originally painted or lacquered or covered with gold leaf. In some instances this must seem hard to believe, especially where the surface appears to have been carved with great care to bring out the full beauty of the grain.

Sometimes the wood was left unpainted. In the Buddhist tradition, this was the case only with certain precious woods, sandalwood or fine fruitwoods (No. 11), but Japanese folk sculpture was often left unpainted; and certain later Chinese carvings, those that were handled almost as though they were semiprecious stone being worked by a lapidary, were also never painted.

Often special craftsmen did the painting, which, in some instances, might take as long as the carving. First, seams and cracks would be covered with fabric or paper, then the entire surface would be covered with gesso. (In Japan, the gesso, called gofun, was made from baked seashells crushed into a powder and mixed with water.) The gesso would then be burnished down and painted. Gold leaf was used extensively, either for covering the entire figure or, in the form of kirikane, for highlighting certain decorative details.

Wood sculpture can be of two basic types. One is carved directly from a single block of wood; the other is joined or fitted together. One might think that the first type would be the earlier; and, in fact, the history of Japanese wood sculpture shows a fairly clear progression from single-block (ichiboku) carving through joined wood constructions of increasing complexity. Yet one of the earliest works in this exhibition, the Ch'ang-sha horse (No. 1), is an example of joined wood while the Kannon by the seventeenth century Japanese monk Enkū (No. 61) is carved from a single block.

Single-block sculpture must contend with some fairly severe limitations. The most obvious of these has to do with size. A single-block sculpture can never be wider than the diameter of the tree from which the block is taken, and monumental sculpture requires a log of enormous proportions. Another drawback of single-block sculpture is its tendency to crack. This can be avoided, but not wholly, by hollowing the sculpture out from inside. It was probably neither of these disadvantages, however, so much as the simple unavailability of appropriate timber that gradually led Chinese and Japanese sculptors to abandon the single-block technique. Prime timber of substantial girth was always at a premium in China and Japan where it was in continual demand for building.

In light of the progressive deforestation of so much of China, one might have thought that the joined wood technique would be found in its most fully developed form there; yet it seems that the most sophisticated examples are to be found in Japan. As mentioned earlier, the development of the technique in Japan, where it is well documented, seems to have followed a fairly logical progression. The earliest stage is well represented by the ninth century Heavenly King *(No. 26)* lent by N. V. Hammer. Note that even in this example the arms (now missing) and that part of the left leg that projects from the central core were carved separately. The rest of the sculpture, however, *was* carved from a single block of wood, and such parts as do project from the block, such as the "tail," tend to be relatively thick and carved parallel to the grain. It should be pointed out that "pure" single-block sculpture, particularly if it is of any size, is extremely rare. Projecting members, such as hands, feet, legs, and arms, are almost always carved separately and added later. A basic reason for this is that wood seldom breaks or splits *across* the grain; it tends to crack *with* it. If a projecting arm were carved from the same block of wood as the body (provided the block had

sufficient diameter to accommodate such a thing!), it would almost certainly break off at the least blow.

The next stage is represented by images which, though carved from a single block, have been extensively hollowed out inside. This stage soon yielded to the earliest form of joined wood construction, represented here by the Torso of a Guardian *(No. 37)*. Now not only were the head and limbs separate but the torso too was divided into two parts, the deeper front and the cover-like back. This allowed the wood to be thinner all the way through and to dry out more completely from all sides, which reduced the likelihood that it would develop cracks.

The earliest verifiable use of the full-fledged *yosegi* technique, as the Japanese call the most highly developed form of joined wood construction, was by the sculptor Jōchō in the great Amida figure in the Byōdō-in, dated 1053. To use this technique, the sculptor must be able to visualize the completed figure in a pre-assembled arrangement of blocks; or, put another way, he must be able to join a number of separate blocks in such a way as to allow him to carve his intended figure from them with a minimum of waste and a maximum of strength. The process, which is an ingenious one, is probably less complicated than it sounds. A good many of the sculptures in this exhibition were constructed according to this method, and a close examination of one or two of them should go far toward elucidating the process.

The portrait of Hōtō Kohushi *(No. 44)* provides a particularly interesting illustration of the *yosegi* technique. The torso, from the shoulders down to the bench (but *not* including the lap), and the arms down to the elbows, form a unit of no less than six separate

7

8

Portrait of Hōtō Kokushi *(Cat. No. 44).*

vertical blocks (or slabs) hollowed out inside and joined together with glue and staples. Several of the staples and seams between the blocks are now quite visible in the sculpture. The forearms, lap, and the overhang of the robes form another unit of *horizontal* blocks joined in the same way. The joined hands are carved from a single piece of wood. The face was probably carved separately, like a mask, then attached to the rest of the head and, with the neck, inserted into the torso. In some sculptures of this kind, however, the head was part of a vertical block or shaft that continued on up from the torso. Some of the joined blocks in a sculpture like this are extremely thin and plank-like. Here, for instance, the two outermost blocks forming the sides of the sleeves are little more than thin plates or caps.

The Chin Dynasty Kuan-yin from the Nelson Gallery *(No. 13)* provides another illustration of the use of the joined wood process. Here too the figure—or the portion of it that remains—seems to have been built up from a series of vertical blocks or slabs. These appear to be solid rather than hollowed out as in Japanese works. Of particular interest is the fact that the left shoulder and arm seem to be part of the same vertical slab as the hip. Note the stout tenon fitting into the fragmentary right arm and the mortise and tenon at the hip. This sculpture provides a rare glimpse of the workaday joinery that, though elsewhere unseen, underlies so many of the works in this exhibition.

Joined wood sculptures were probably actually carved in pre-assembled units, which could be disassembled if necessary for close work on specific details. The face was almost always a separate mask-like piece capable of being held and worked in the hand before being fitted into place. The crystal eyes, which are such a life-like feature of later Japanese sculpture, were, of course, inserted from behind.

The perfection of the joined wood process not only made it possible to produce works of surprising lightness considering their size but—of even greater significance—it immeasurably expanded the plastic possibilities of the medium. Released from the imprisoning confines of a single block, wood became every bit as flexible a means of expression as bronze or dry lacquer. The dramatic realism of Kamakura Period sculpture would have been inconceivable without this development.

CHINA

EASTERN CHOU DYNASTY 771-256 B.C.

Period of the Spring and Autumn Annals, 722-481 B.C.

Period of the Warring States, 481-221 B.C.

CH'IN DYNASTY 221-206 B.C.

HAN DYNASTY 206 B.C.-A.D. 220

THREE KINGDOMS 220-280

SIX DYNASTIES 220-589

SUI DYNASTY 581-618

T'ANG DYNASTY 618-906

FIVE DYNASTIES 907-960

SUNG DYNASTY 960-1279

Northern Sung Dynasty 960-1127　　　LIAO 907-1125

Southern Sung Dynasty 1127-1279　　CHIN 1115-1234

YÜAN DYNASTY 1280-1368

MING DYNASTY 1368-1644

CH'ING DYNASTY 1644-1912

JAPAN

NARA PERIOD 645-794

HEIAN PERIOD 794-1185

Early Heian, or Jōgan, 794-897

Late Heian, or Fujiwara, 897-1185

KAMAKURA PERIOD 1185-1333

MUROMACHI (ASHIKAGA) PERIOD 1392-1568

MOMOYAMA PERIOD 1568-1615

EDO (TOKUGAWA) PERIOD 1615-1867

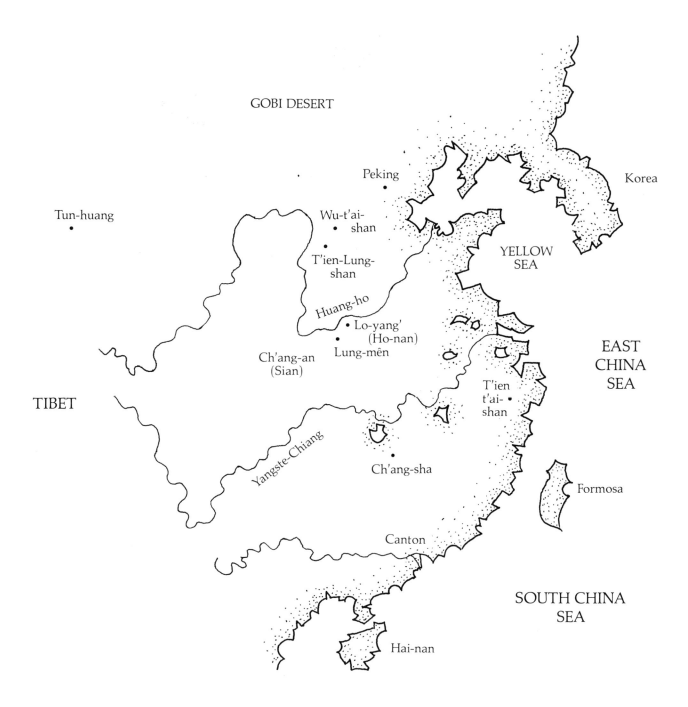

GOBI DESERT

Peking

Korea

Tun-huang

Wu-t'ai-
shan

YELLOW
SEA

T'ien-Lung-
shan

Huang-ho

Lo-yang'
(Ho-nan)

EAST
CHINA
SEA

Ch'ang-an
(Sian)

Lung-mên

TIBET

T'ien
t'ai-
shan

Yangste-Chiang

Ch'ang-sha

Formosa

Canton

SOUTH CHINA
SEA

Hai-nan

SEA OF
JAPAN

Kyoto

Kamakura

Nara

PACIFIC
OCEAN

The earliest known examples of Chinese wood carving came from an area north and south of the central Yangtze, the region that formed the ancient Kingdom of Ch'u, one of the largest of the "warring states" into which China was divided during the latter half of the Chou Dynasty (1122-222 B.C.). These objects, most of which share a striking family resemblance, are presumed to date from the fourth and third centuries B.C. and are remarkably well preserved considering their age and the fact that they were buried underground in a very humid climate. That they survived at all would seem nothing short of miraculous were it not for recent excavations that have clarified Ch'u burial practices.

The people of Ch'u obviously took great care to ensure the preservation of their tombs. Though details varied, most burials followed a common formula. The tomb itself consisted of a series of wooden coffins, perhaps as many as six, nested one inside the other and placed at the bottom of a deep, rectangular pit, the floor of which was often plastered with limey white clay. The outermost coffin rested on stout, transverse timbers resembling railroad ties and was solidly constructed of thick planks caulked with clay. Compartments for funerary objects were left between this (or the next) coffin and the others. The inner coffins might be painted or lacquered. In even the oldest sites, both outer and inner coffins are carefully fitted and joined, bespeaking an advanced level of craftsmanship.

Apparently the most important factor determining the preservation of these tombs was the thickness of the clay used to caulk and encase them. In some of the better preserved tombs, the clay was as much as 60 to 100 cms. thick. Sometimes an inner layer of charcoal was used in addition. The efficacy of such means was demonstrated in spectacular fashion with the discovery of the tomb of Lady Tai in which burial offerings of meat and vegetables were found virtually intact and the body was so well preserved that an autopsy could be performed on it. Though the tomb dates from the early years of the Han Dynasty (206-B.C.—221 A.D.), hence after the fall of Ch'u, the method of burial clearly followed Ch'u formulas and the tomb furniture was little different from that found at earlier sites.

Among the burial objects were 162 wooden figures. Some of these, though better preserved, bear a strong resemblance to the wooden figurines in this exhibition. Even in this one burial, however, there is considerable variation in the degree and quality of carving from one group of figures to another. Some look rigid and tubular, others show greater animation; some are painted, others are clothed. Obviously, with articles as mass-produced and conventional as these, a more primitive look does not necessarily mean an earlier date. Without gainsaying their charm, it must be said that most of these figurines are in no way indicative of the level of skill attained by Ch'u craftsmen. Recent excavations of Ch'u sites have yielded wood carvings of incredible fluency and polish. One of the most remarkable of these was a small openwork screen with birds, writhing snakes, and bounding deer carved with great freedom and in naturalistic detail!

Were wooden figurines like these in this exhibition made elsewhere in China or was their use restricted to the Kingdom of Ch'u? This is a question that still cannot be answered with any certainty. It is unlikely that wooden burial objects were limited to this one area, however, particularly in light of the fact that China was much more extensively forested at this period, even in the North.

These Ch'u burial figures do seem to have certain stylistic features in common, the most marked of which is a preference for elegantly attenuated forms; but whether this is sufficient basis for speaking of a "Chu style" remains an open question. Early records speak of the Ch'u as a highly literate, cultivated people possessed by a belief in ghosts and divination. They developed a sophisticated silk industry and probably produced more lacquer than any other area of China at the time. They were said to be partial to an elaborate form of calligraphy known as bird script. There seems to be every reason to suspect the existence of a distinctive Ch'u sensibility, which may well have expressed itself in a special Ch'u style.

[1] Annette L. Juliano, "Three Large Ch'u Graves Recently Excavated in the Chiangling District of Hupei Province," *Artibus Asiae*, XXXIV, 1972.

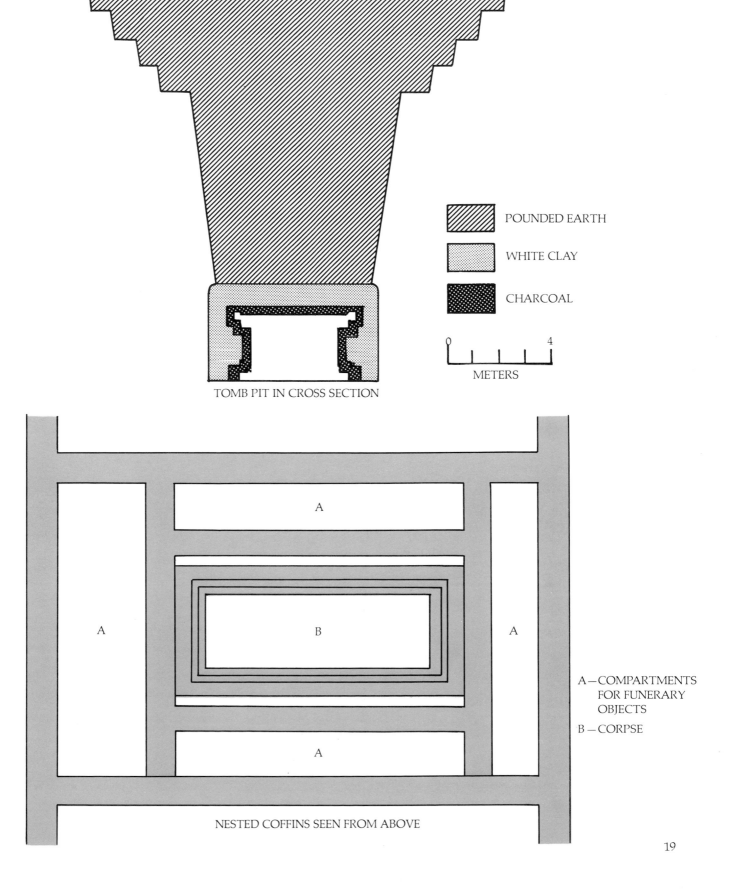

POUNDED EARTH

WHITE CLAY

CHARCOAL

0   4

METERS

TOMB PIT IN CROSS SECTION

A

A   B   A

A

A—COMPARTMENTS
    FOR FUNERARY
    OBJECTS

B—CORPSE

NESTED COFFINS SEEN FROM ABOVE

1. HORSE

Late Eastern Chou Dynasty, Warring States Period,
early 3rd century B.C.
Height: 70.5 cm.
Portland Art Museum, Portland, Oregon   40.28

Nothing comparable to this horse has yet come to light in any of the controlled excavations undertaken in China since the early 1950's, so our attribution to the Kingdom of Ch'u must be considered tentative at best. The piece is reputed to come from Ch'ang-sha, however — the site of numerous Ch'u finds — and both the condition and the obvious age of the wood as well as the angular, attenuated style of carving would seem to bear this out.

For all its stylized nature, the horse conveys a remarkable sense of alert animal vitality. This is perhaps as much due to its erect stance — its neck pulled back, its mouth open baring teeth and gums — as to the sensitive attention paid to details such as the hooves, the pasterns, and the hocks. It is put together from eight separate pieces of wood (head, neck, body, four legs, and tail) presumably joined by mortises and tenons. The grain runs parallel to the length of each piece and so is vertical in the legs and neck, horizontal in the body and head. The body still retains some of the rectangular character of the block of wood from which it was carved, particularly underneath, where it is almost flat. The legs, viewed straight on, are extremely thin and slat-like. Perhaps the most interesting part of the animal is the head. The red

outlines of a bridle are visible under strong light, and the inside of the mouth is a paler red. There may well have been ears, now broken off, at the back of the head; if so, they were probably part of the same piece of wood, not carved separately and set in.

There are signs of modern repairs at all the major joints, but vestiges of the original surface — a much-worn brownish black which may be lacquer — cover extensive areas elsewhere, particularly on the body.

Images of horses have occupied an important place in Chinese tomb furniture from at least the Han Dynasty on. Westerners are probably most familiar with the splendidly caparisoned ceramic steeds of T'ang burials, but the famous "flying" bronze horse of Kansu is another example of the type. The horse became a symbol of nobility and excellence in later Chinese art and literature. It is tempting to see the beginnings of this concept here.

There is another, quite similar horse, also purported to come from Ch'ang-sha, in a private collection in Chicago. Max Loehr, in his catalogue of the Singer Collection, reproduces a painted wood horse of about the same period but which is much more rounded and seems closer to ceramic examples.

2. HUMAN FIGURINE
Late Eastern Chou Dynasty, Warring States Period,
4th-3rd century B.C.
Height: 59.1 cm.
*The Metropolitan Museum of Art, New York. Gift of
Mathias Komor, 1948*

This figure, though quite different from the other Ch'u figures in
this exhibition, is representative of a type of which there are
numerous examples in Western collections. Figures of this type
apparently all once belonged to a single set which was dispersed
in 1949.

The mouth is raised and squared off rather than pointed at the
ends. The ears are flat and almost seem to be (though they are
not) separate wedges of wood tenoned into the head. The eyebrows
are long and drawn together over the top of the nose which
forms a broad triangle. These are all standard features of the type.
The collar is painted rather than carved as in *Nos. 4 and 5.* The
hands, which are missing—as they almost always are in these
figures—would have been tenoned into the mortises cut into the
tops of the sleeves. The sleeves themselves seem to droop, pouch-
like, at the elbows. The tip of an undergarment (or, if the outer robe
is wrapped, perhaps merely the inside edge of that robe itself)
emerges from below the front of the robe, and below this is what
seems to be a baggy pantaloon-like garment. The figure stands
on two flat, rectangular boards (possibly modern restorations)
which seem to represent shoes or sandals.

3. FEMALE ATTENDANT OR MOURNER

Late Eastern Chou Dynasty, Warring States Period,
4th-3rd century B.C.
Height: 52.1 cm.
Asian Art Museum of San Francisco, the Avery Brundage Collection

This figure, assumed to be that of a woman, is as different from
the preceding piece in almost as many respects as it is similar to it.
Perhaps the greatest difference, apart from the obvious one of
condition, is in its relative proportions. The neck is shorter and
the shoulders broader and rounder. In this respect, it is clearly more
realistic. The head, on the other hand, with its short but extraor-
dinarily wide forehead, seems curiously stylized.

   Another marked difference between the two figures is in their
style of carving. What is sharp and angular in the previous one
becomes soft and rounded here, an effect that is only emphasized
by the abraded condition of the piece.

   The surface shows traces of black lacquer. On one shoulder
and under the right ear are patches of hair or fur that might possibly
be the remains of a wig.

23

4. FIGURE WITH SWORD

Late Eastern Chou Dynasty, Warring States Period,
4th-3rd century B.C., from Ch'ang-sha
Height: 49.5 cm.
Cleveland Museum of Art. Purchase from the J. H. Wade Fund

This figure, which seems to be a warrior or guard in the act of
striding forth, grasping a sword in his right hand, presents a
striking contrast to the majority of Ch'u burial figures, which
depict servants or attendants in relatively passive roles. There are
other differences too, of course, notably in the extent and
descriptive detail of the carving. Features are carved which in
other figures would be painted or perhaps merely implied. Yet, for
all these differences, the family resemblance with other Ch'u
figures (*No. 2*, for instance) is apparent in the general proportions
as well as such details as the elongated neck and flat head. The
head and neck and two legs seem to be carved from separate
pieces of wood.

The figure wears an interesting tunic-like garment with a high,
stiff collar and puffy shoulders. Extensive traces of the original
pigments remain, including a particularly brilliant vermilion in
the recessed band at the bottom of the garment.

5. ATTENDANT FIGURE

Late Eastern Chou Dynasty, Warring States Period,
5th-3rd century B.C.
Height: 51.1 cm.
William Rockhill Nelson Gallery of Art—
Atkins Museum of Fine Arts, Kansas City, Missouri.
Gift of Mary and Vincent Price

This tall, attenuated figure emerged from burial with the raised
grain and weathered appearance one associates with drift-
wood, giving it an air of ghostly refinement that seems strangely
moving. The eyes and mouth have all but disappeared, and the
brow lacks the sharp undercutting seen in the previous figures.
On the other hand, the jaw, chin, neck, and collar are not unlike
those in *No. 4*, and the two figures also seem related in the degree to
which details are rendered by carving. The left arm hangs down,
the sleeve merging into the expanding skirt of the robe. The right
arm, broken off at the wrist, extends out as though to hold or
present something. The head is carved from a separate piece of
wood. The costume is unusual; its most remarkable feature being
the parallel diagonal bands or overlapping folds at the bottom.

TWO DANCING FIGURES

6. Late Eastern Chou Dynasty, Warring States Period,
4th-3rd century B.C.
Height: 34.6 cm.
Seattle Art Museum. Eugene Fuller Memorial Collection

7. Late Eastern Chou Dynasty, Warring States Period,
4th-3rd century B.C., from Ch'ang-sha
Height: 35.6 cm.
Mr. and Mrs. James W. Alsdorf, Winnetka, Illinois

Though the motif of the female dancer with long, fluttering sleeves occurs repeatedly throughout the history of Chinese art, and burial figures of such dancers are often found among the tomb furnishings of later dynasties, these two figures—both reputedly from the Ch'ang-sha region and both, therefore, very possibly dating from the fourth or third century B.C.—may well represent one of the earliest appearances of this theme.

Hand and arm movements have always been important to the Chinese dancer, who uses long sleeves in place of scarves or streamers to give sweep and elegance to her gestures.

At first glance these two dancers may seem totally different from the other Ch'ang-sha figures exhibited here. Certainly they have none of the stiff, angular quality of *No. 2;* and their sweeping gestures and bell-shaped skirts give them an appearance of amplitude—of expansiveness even—that definitely sets them apart from *any* of the other figures, almost all of which seem thin and columnar by comparison. Yet even these two dancers are really very thin, astonishingly so when seen in profile; and the faces have the broad foreheads and pointed chins seen in all these pieces.

The features in *No. 6* have all but disappeared, and the piece has some of the same soft, weathered quality that was seen in *No. 3.* The eyes in *No. 7* may well have been recarved after excavation.

8. A PAIR OF FEMALE ATTENDANTS

Sui Dynasty, *ca.* 600 A.D.
Height: 47 cm.
William Rockhill Nelson Gallery of Art—
Atkins Museum of Fine Arts, Kansas City, Missouri

Similar figures, but of ceramic rather than wood, have long been familiar to students of Far Eastern art. It is an interesting commentary on the relative durability of the two materials that hardly any other wood burial figures of this period have survived.

The two women stand as though at attention, holding out small, jar-like objects in front of them. Are they attendants at a banquet or participants in some stately procession or ritual? Whatever the role they represent, they remind one in many respects of the ceramic images of male court officials, also found in pairs and equally ceremonious in pose, that are so common among Wei, Sui and T'ang burial figures. The greater tensile strength of wood allows for projections and undercutting, however, that would be all but impossible with clay. Note the slender wrists and the long, hollowed-out sleeves.

One of these two figures was too fragile to be included in the exhibition. The exhibited figure is shown in the larger photograph at right.

The history of Chinese wood sculpture is to such a large extent the history of Chinese *Buddhist* wood sculpture that it is impossible to understand without some knowledge of Buddhism itself, particulary Mahāyāna Buddhism, which is the form that faith took in China.

Central to all Buddhist thought is the conviction that nothing is permanent, not even the self or soul, and that suffering, which is caused by attachment, by resisting the inevitability of change, is unavoidable. Escape from the treadmill of ceaseless change and suffering is possible, but only through enlightenment. The basic teachings of Buddhism concern the means of attaining this enlightenment. It should be pointed out that the very name *Buddha* means, in Sanskrit, "the enlightened one."

Very early in its history, Buddhism separated into two great streams. One, Hīnayāna Buddhism, the "Lesser Vehicle," may represent an earlier phase of the religion in which the mystical elements are minimized. More literal in its application of the Buddha's teachings, it concentrates on personal salvation through monastic discipline. Emphasizing the difficulty of spiritual attainment, its ideal is the *arhat*, the monk who has achieved sainthood.

Mahāyāna Buddhism, the "Greater Vehicle," believes in the inherent "Buddha nature" of all sentient beings. Its ideal is universal compassion as exemplified in the bodhisattva who vows to save all living things. The mystical elements in Mahāyāna Buddhism are strong. The historical Buddha, Gautama Shakyamuni, is seen as only one of a succession of Buddhas through time, each a particular manifestation of the eternal Buddha nature; as such, he often seems eclipsed by Maitreya, the future Buddha, or Amitabha, the Buddha of Infinite Light. With its message of universal salvation and its vast pantheon of compassionate Buddhas and bodhisattvas, Mahāyāna Buddhism was capable of stirring the religious imagination of its followers in a way that few other creeds have ever matched. Only a fraction of the Buddhist art produced in China still survives, but the staggering complexity and sheer volume of what remains attests to the power of the faith that inspired it.

Much of the direct inspiration for this art came from sacred literature. The bulk of this literature is enormous. The most recent edition of the Chinese canon runs to 100 volumes of 1000 closely printed pages each. Some notion of the complexity of Chinese Buddhism can be gained from this fact alone. The fact that scriptures continued to be accepted into the canon until quite late points up another aspect of Chinese Buddhism, its tolerance, its ability to accept new doctrines as long as these were not in conflict with the basic premises of the faith. Scholars have often written about the syncretic tendencies of Buddhism. Those tendencies are definitely present in Chinese Buddhism.

The first Buddhist missionaries reached China some time during the Han Dynasty; precisely when is uncertain, but perhaps as early as 2 B.C. The new faith made little headway at first. China already possessed two native systems of belief, Confucianism and Taoism; Confucianism, in particular, with its emphasis on the family and service to the state, was bound to be hostile to a creed espousing celibacy and withdrawal from the world. The fall of the Han Dynasty in 220 A.D. and the ensuing turmoil and despair, however, created a situation in which the otherworldly values of Buddhism gained a new appeal, and the number of conversions rapidly in-

33

creased. The greatest gains were made in the North, which was subject to continuous alien rule, though under different dynasties, from 316 to 581 A.D. Among the various Northern dynasties, the Wei were particularly lavish in their patronage of the new religion, and to this day the stupendous rock carvings and cave complexes of Yün-kang and Lung-mên attest to the fervour of their new-found faith.

It was also a Northern Wei ruler, however, who, in 446, instituted the first major persecution of Buddhism in China. Such persecutions—there were two others of equal severity in subsequent dynasties—succeeded in destroying the Buddhist-inspired art and architecture of entire periods. Works of wood and metal were, of course, particularly vulnerable. What survived was either sculpture of stone or small portable icons of bronze. The persecution of 446 did not last long, however, and by 494, when the Northern Wei moved their capital to Lo-yang, the dynastic patronage of Buddhism had reached new levels of extravagance. Literally thousands of temples were constructed, over a thousand in the capital city itself. Among these was one, the Yung-ning Temple, which—if contemporary accounts are to be credited—probably exceeded in grandeur any other Buddhist edifice ever built.

In 534 the Dynasty collapsed, and that same year the Yung-ning Temple, hit by lightning, burned to the ground. Within little more than a decade, hardly one of the thousand temples of Lo-yang remained. Clearly periodic persecutions were not the only factors adversely affecting the survival of Buddhist antiquities in China. Natural disasters such as fire, floods and earthquakes, or invasions, and the violent collapse of dynasties could be equally devastating.

Chinese Buddhism did, however, have to weather one further episode of persecution before emerging into the period of its greatest activity and achievement during the seventh century. This was the suppression of 574-577 under the Emperor Wu of the Northern Chou Dynasty. Like the persecutions of 446, it was confined to the North.

The re-unification of China under the Sui Dynasty in 581 and the further consolidation of the country under the T'ang in 618 set the stage for the glorious cultural full noon of the next two centuries. It was a period of unparalleled expansiveness and confidence. Never before had Chinese culture been so cosmopolitan. The streets of Ch'ang-an, the capital city, were thronged with visitors from as far away as Persia, and Nestorian Christians rubbed shoulders with Buddhist student-monks from Japan. Chinese cultural hegemony extended from Japan on the east across Central Asia to Samarkand and Bokhara in the west; and fashions started in Ch'ang-an were picked up, in a surprisingly short time, at way stations all along this band of influence. So strong was the Chinese influence in Japan that Nara, the capital from 710 to 784, was virtually a miniature duplicate of Ch'ang-an.

For Buddhism, the seventh century was a period of renewed contact with the sources of the religion in India. Hardy pilgrims made the arduous overland trek across Central Asia to Northern India and such centers of Buddhist learning as Nālandā; others journeyed by sea. The texts and images they brought back contributed to the intellectual ferment that was taking place in Chinese Buddhism at the time.

In the arts, too, the results of renewed contact with India soon became apparent. Sculpture loses the ethereal quality it had earlier (especially under the Northern Wei) in exchange for a new weightiness and sense of actual physical presence. Drapery begins to conform to the outlines of the body underneath, instead of going its independent way, and the body itself is rendered with greater freedom. The result is, at times, a sensual, almost voluptuous, quality that is totally new in Chinese sculpture.

The seventh century saw Buddhism reach the height of its prestige and popularity under imperial patronage. It also saw the growing popularity of the Pure Land sect, which promised rebirth in the Western Paradise (or Pure Land) to those who invoked the name of the Buddha Amitabha. By the late T'ang Dynasty this undemanding doctrine had attracted more followers than any other, and to this day it is the dominant form of Buddhism in both China and Japan.

Ch'an Buddhism (better known in the West by its Japanese name, Zen) also began to attract increasing attention at this time. Stressing the master-pupil relationship and what it called "a direct transmission from mind to mind," Ch'an had little use for the scriptures and icons that played such an important role in the devotions of the other sects. In one sense intensely practical, it concentrated on the means of attaining enlightenment in this world and was not interested in the promise of paradise after death. It produced a series of extraordinary teachers, men whose enlightenment had been recognized by their predecessors in a line that was traced back directly to the reputed founder, Bodhidharma, who was said to have arrived in China in 520 A.D.

The Ch'an sect developed its own unique imagery centering on the cryptic utterances and seemingly outlandish deeds of its patriarchs, whose intentional eccentricities were their chosen, if unorthodox, means of instruction. This interest in extreme forms of individualism eventually found expression in a school of portraiture that had an enormous influence on the subsequent course of Chinese and Japanese sculpture.

Another form of Buddhism that was to have a marked, if relatively brief, impact on the arts arrived in China early in the eighth century. Known as Tantric, or Esoteric, Buddhism, it represented a relatively late phase of the religion in India, after it had already incorporated numerous Hindu elements. With its awesome pantheon of many-armed, multiheaded, often ferocious deities and its ritual use of hand signs (mudra), spells (mantra), and mystical diagrams (mandalas), it seems to have appealed only briefly to the Chinese. Japanese monks visiting China towards the end of the eighth century were attracted to it, however, and introduced it to Japan, where the Esoteric Shingon and Tendai sects continue to flourish even today. The Tibetan form of Tantric Buddhism, Lamaism, was introduced to North China during the Mongol Yüan Dynasty, and Lamaist Temples in Peking continued to receive imperial patronage up until the revolution of 1911.

In 845 Chinese Buddhism suffered the most drastic persecution of its history. This time it was not confined to only a single section of the country, and it dealt the religion a blow from which it never fully recovered. The richest and most venerable temples were precisely the most severely hit. All images of bronze or precious metals were confiscated to be melted down for coin. Bells suffered the same fate. Monks and nuns by the thousands were forced to return to lay life. The destruction of icons and ritual implements must have been enormous. It is little wonder that most of the surviving Buddhist wood sculpture dates from after 845.

Only two sects, Pure Land and Ch'an, managed to recover from this disaster with their followings relatively intact. Pure Land beliefs were so entrenched at the popular level that they were relatively unaffected by moves aimed against the clerical establishment; and the leading Ch'an monasteries were concentrated away from the metropolitan centers, in regions where the power of the government was less secure, and so were able to escape the full brunt of the persecution.

As might be expected, almost all subsequent Buddhist sculpture in China bears the impress of one or the other of these two sects, though the increasing influence of folk beliefs, tinged with Taoism, also becomes apparent later. The austere or otherworldly icons of earlier periods are replaced with images of more immediate, popular appeal. Kuan-yin seems to be particularly favored, and increasingly it is the feminine, more alluring aspect of this Bodhisattva that is emphasized. Portraits of monks, of considerable realism, and often of great intensity of expression as well, reflect the continuity of Ch'an traditions. Ch'an influence is also apparent in the numerous caricatures of Arhats *(Nos. 14 and 16)* and in the development of the popular image of Pu-tai *(No. 19)*.

The word "temple" has been used with great frequency here, yet in a Buddhist context it has a rather special meaning. In English, the word suggests a single, usually rather monumental, edifice; in Chinese and Japanese usage, it generally means a complex of buildings, customarily surrounded by walls and entered through a series of gates. The orientation is invariably to the south, with the chief access being from that direction, a layout influenced by the ancient Chinese belief that evil influences approach from the northeast. The most distinctive buildings within such a complex are the tall, tower-like pagoda and the "Golden Hall" in which the principal icons are housed; but a fully developed temple, particularly of the earlier periods, might include any number of additional special-purpose buildings, such as sūtra repositiories, bell towers, lecture halls, and refectories. Perhaps the word "monastery" would more appropriately describe such temple complexes, which invariably included living quarters.

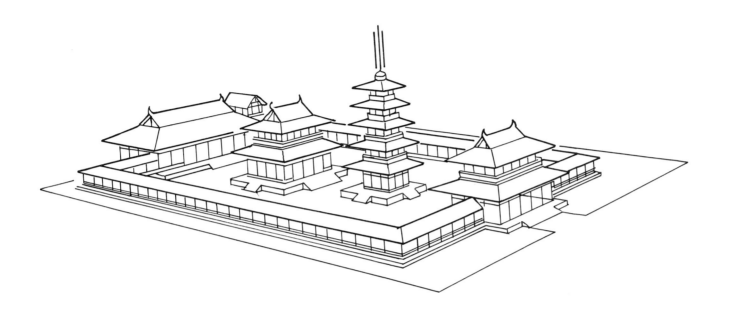

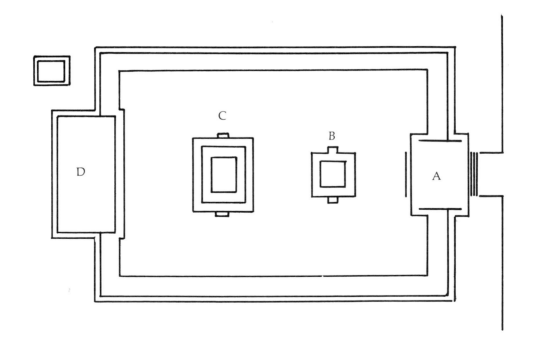

A, MAIN SOUTH GATE   B, PAGODA   C, GOLDEN HALL   D, LECTURE HALL

9. ELEVEN-HEADED KUAN-YIN

Early T'ang Dynasty, late seventh century
Height: 62.9 cm.
Cleveland Museum of Art. Purchase, John L. Severance Fund

Images of the Eleven-headed Kuan-yin, an esoteric form of the great Bodhisattva of Compassion, Avalokitesvara, enjoyed only a brief period of popularity in China and may even have become obsolete after the ninth century. By contrast, such images continued to be made in great numbers in Japan until well into the Kamakura Period (1185-1392). Of the few Chinese examples that have survived, almost all are of stone. As mentioned earlier, Chinese wood sculpture of the T'ang Dynasty is exceedingly rare. It seems little short of miraculous that an image as unusual as this should have been among the few examples preserved.

The image has been dated to the early T'ang Dynasty, which would probably place it in the seventh century and make it among one of the earliest known representatives of this form of the Bodhisattva. Several features support such an early date. One of the most important of these is the striking contrast between the rich detail of the heavy pendants and necklaces with the shallow carving of the rest of the figure, a trait typical of the sculpture of the Northern Ch'i (550-577) and Sui (581-618) Dynasties. The straightforward posture and almost rigid hieratic stance seem at a far remove from the usual T'ang *contrapposto*, and the "fish-tail" projections at the hem line of the robe (the appearance of which may have been altered by restoration) may even refer back to

mannerisms typical of the late Wei Dynasty (535-554). The coronets or crowns on the subsidiary heads are also of a type primarily found in late Wei Dynasty sculpture. Other features, however, point to the seventh century or later. The most important of these is the marked fleshiness of the work. The face, with its fine, arched eyebrows, heavy eyelids, and full lips, has the plumpness, dumpiness even, that one associates with the mid to late seventh century. The facial type is close to that found in a stone stele of this deity dated 691. Such conflicting stylistic elements suggest that the sculpture might have been carved during the late seventh century, but in a conservative tradition and for use by a specific cult.

Images of the Eleven-headed Kuan-yin display considerable variation in the arrangement of the subsidiary heads. This arrangement, with four heads at either side, one at the back, and a tenth head at the top, is encountered only infrequently. The fact that all the heads are of benign countenance is even more unusual. According to the standard iconography, three of the heads should have angry faces, three others should have tusks, and one, at the back, should be laughing.

The figure is remarkably intact, with the exception of the repair at the hemline mentioned earlier.

38

10. KUAN-YIN SEATED IN ROYAL EASE
Five Dynasties Period, 10th century
Height: 43.2 cm.
The Denver Art Museum. Walter C. Mead Collection

For all its languor, there is something more than a little imperious about this figure. It is seated in a pose, the Indian name of which, appropriately enough, is *maharaja-lalitasana*, "royal ease." It seems far removed from the preceding figure *(No. 9)*, even though it represents the same Bodhisattva (albeit in a different manifestation) and may be only several centuries later in date. However, while the Eleven-headed Kuan-yin all but disappeared in China after the ninth century, the Kuan-yin Seated in Royal Ease became increasingly popular. This form of the Bodhisattva is generally associated with the Sung Dynasty (960-1279), and numerous images of it dating from that period, or a little later, can be found in Western collections. Here the face, with its high, broad cheeks, is a classic T'ang type, however, and the body, too, with its high, narrow waist, follows a T'ang formula perfected in the eighth century. The entire figure has a sense of weight and definition that is lost in later examples, particularly in those where the drapery becomes over-elaborate and confused. Here the scarf, draped over the right arm and falling to the top of the dais parallel with the left, creates a delicate counterpoint that enhances one's sense of the underlying structure of these limbs. There is something particularly convincing about the way the figure casually leans back, bracing itself with its left arm, its right arm resting on its upraised right knee. The left leg is pendant, the foot resting on a projecting socle in the form of a lotus flower.

The long tresses of hair which fall onto the shoulders where they divide into separate strands are common to all the images of Kuan-yin shown here. The high topknot, however, is distinctive, as is the simple tiara, even though the frontlet does bear the image of Amida, the Buddha almost always associated with Kuan-yin in this way.

The hexagonal dais is unusual. Most such figures were originally seated on pedestals simulating the rocky shore of Potala, the Bodhisattva's fabled mountain home in the Southern Seas.

Much of the figure is still covered with what appears to be the original polychrome, white for the body, greyish white for the drapery and vermilion, pink, and green for the jewelry.

11. POTALA KUAN-YIN

Five Dynasties Period, 10th century
Height: 15.2 cm.
Cleveland Museum of Art. Mrs. A. Dean Perry Collection

This fragile little fruitwood figure has been dated to the tenth
century on the basis of its resemblance to similar figures found
deposited in one of the principal icons of the Kuang-hsiao-ssu
in Canton.

    The figure has some of the daintiness and refinement of ivory
carving. The neck seems impossibly slender, and there is little
articulation or sense of fleshiness to the body. The left arm, for
instance, seems to have little more substance than an empty sleeve,
and the left leg is curiously foreshortened.

    Some of the same fey delicacy applies to the figure's adornment.
Flowery streamers, or garlands, hang from its shoulders and are
draped over the right arm and upraised knee. The lacy pierced-
work crown is particularly distinctive.

    The bulk of the hair is drawn up into a topknot surmounted
by the crown, but loose tresses—now broken from the head—
fall down in long strands over the shoulders where they mingle
with the streamers.

12. STANDING FIGURE (TORSO OF A BODHISATTVA)
Five Dynasties Period, 10th century
Height: 39.3 cm.
Mr. and Mrs. James W. Alsdorf, Winnetka, Illinois

Though lacking its head, forearms, and feet, this small figure is almost certainly that of a bodhisattva and very likely, in fact, represents Kuan-yin. The stance is dignified and generous, one leg placed slightly behind the other, the arms extended away from the body. The figure wears a scarf thrown shawl-like over its shoulders; and a sash, looped under itself at the left, is drawn diagonally across its chest. The only other adornment is a heavy necklace, with a massive pendant, though originally, chains or cords, now almost entirely broken off, once hung from the necklace as well. Perhaps the most distinctive feature of this sculpture is the skirt with its loose overhang and numerous loose, parallel folds. A roll of excess fabric at the waist hangs down in front over a sash tied in a neat bow.

This figure has been attributed to the tenth century, and a comparison with *No. 17*, dated 1282, is interesting in this regard. This figure is much more restrained than *No. 17;* there is less twist to the body, and the drapery shows less movement, less animation. Clearly it is the more conservative figure of the two. Yet other details, such as the roll of excess fabric at the waist and the position of the arms, seem remarkably close. One can even detect in this figure the first signs of that trough-like depression of the skirt between the legs that is such a distinctive feature of early Yüan Dynasty sculpture.

13. KUAN-YIN

Chin Dynasty (1115-1234)
Height: 63.5 cm.
William Rockhill Nelson Gallery of Art—Atkins Museum of
Fine Arts, Kansas City, Missouri. Nelson Fund

The extraordinary strength and clarity of the carving of this piece
is apparent even in its present fragmentary state. The sharp folds
of the drapery stand out in high relief, and strands of hair flow
back across the shoulder in vigorous ripples. The length of the torso
is emphasized by the long face and the height of the upswept hair
behind the tall headdress. The vigor of the piece and the erect
bearing seem difficult to reconcile with the fact that, when
complete, the figure was seated in the posture of "royal ease";
yet a comparison with *No. 10* will readily show that this was the
case. (Note the exposed mortise and tenon at the point where the
left thigh would have projected from the hip.) Clearly this
sculpture has little of the languor found in so many of these
seated images of Kuan-yin.

A scarf is draped simply over the shoulders and a sash, tied
in a single loop, falls across the chest. There are none of the
fluttering entanglements of scarves and sashes seen in other works
of the same approximate date. The skirt is secured with a narrow
sash, tied in a firm bow, over which hangs a fold of excess fabric.
The Standing Kuan-yin of 1282 *(No. 17)* shows a very similar
treatment of this same feature. This sculpture, however, probably
dates from over a century earlier. It is thought to come from
Shansi, a region particularly rich in fine examples of wood sculpture
of this period.

HEADS OF THREE LOHAN

Lohan is the Chinese word for *arhat*, the "perfected saint" of Hīnayāna Buddhism who has put an end to his cravings and all but attained nirvana. In the Mahāyāna tradition, lohans (*rakan* in Japanese) are seen as monks of extraordinary spiritual attainment and superhuman powers. In art, they tend to be represented as craggy-featured ascetics, their bodies wasted through the practice of life-long austerities. Their exotic, often outlandish appearance points to their Indian origin, as disciples of Shakyamuni; but such exaggerated features as long eyebrows or domed heads probably derive from analogy with the Taoist Immortals, with whom, in China, they were sometimes confused.

Lohans were rarely, if ever, depicted in isolation but appeared in groups of four, sixteen, eighteen, 500, 1000, or even 5000. Though lists giving the names and attributes of individual lohans do exist, the lack of uniformity and vagueness of these lists usually makes identification difficult.

14. Sung Dynasty (960-1279)
Height: 47 cm.
Asian Art Museum of San Francisco, the Avery Brundage Collection

This lohan is portrayed as an old man with a protruding forehead, jutting chin, huge ears (a sign of superior wisdom), and long, rippling eyebrows—the last two strands on each side curling around above the ears and behind to the back of the head. All of the features are deeply undercut and exaggerated and treated in a rather humorous, if not satirical manner.

Carved from a single block of wood, the head has a cavity hollowed out inside, accessible through a rectangular opening at the back. At one time, items of religious significance or magical import may have been placed inside, but now the cavity is empty. Patches of cloth, lacquer, and red pigment still remain on the head which once would have fit into an opening at the top of the torso of a figure.

As mentioned before, the iconographical descriptions of lohans are rather confusing, and it seems that this example might represent either A-shih-to, the "Invincible" or "Unconquered," Pin-tu-lo po-to-shê, the "Long-eyebrowed Monk," or Yin-chie-to-tsun-chê, all of whom are described as possessing exceptionally long eyebrows, perhaps the most noteworthy feature of this sculpture.

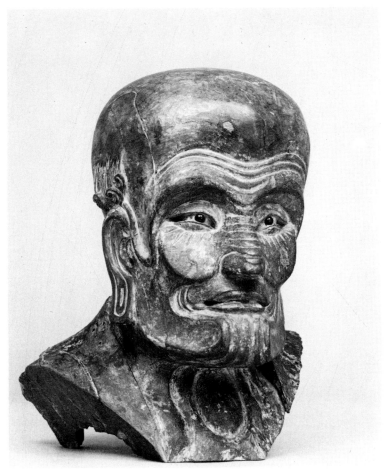

15. Ming Dynasty, 14th-15th century
Height: 29.2 cm.
Asian Art Museum of San Francisco, the Avery Brundage Collection

Though this could almost be taken as a simple portrait of a monk, it probably represents one of the lohans. Cleanly shaven with furrowed brows and a scowling countenance, he is depicted with his mouth open, revealing both his top row of teeth and his tongue which are carved out of the block of wood. The modeling of this head is exceptionally fine with subtle transitions in the musculature, indicating careful observation and knowledge of anatomy by the artist. The eyes are carefully and rather sharply articulated with the pupil and white of the eye carved directly from the block.

There is a deep hole on the top of the head which meets a wide crack in the back, inside of which the wood is extremely soft. Traces of yellow paint remain on the back of the head.

16. Ming Dynasty (1368-1644)
Height: 27.9 cm.
Art Institute of Chicago. Gift of Mr. and Mrs. James W. Alsdorf

This head, with its sharp carving and rather mannered depiction of anatomical details, seems to mark a somewhat later development in the depiction of lohans in Chinese sculpture. A powerful work, the facial features and structure have become standardized to the point where they have become icons in themselves and have lost their credibility as actual human features. This is particularly noticeable in the ridges across the nose, the grooves across the forehead and on the chin, the curious treatment of the hair above the ears and the almost ray-like treatment of the lashes below the eyes.

There is a serious, determined, and rather calm look on the face of this lohan which contrasts with the grimacing, scowling countenance of the previous piece.

47

17. STANDING KUAN-YIN

Yüan Dynasty, 1282 A.D.
Height: 99.5 cm.
The Metropolitan Museum of Art, New York.
Purchase, Joseph Pulitzer Bequest, 1934

The image of Amitabha on the tiara of this figure and the strands of hair falling across its shoulders identify it as the Great Bodhisattva of Compassion, Kuan-yin. An inscription on the inside of the removable back panel covering the "treasure chamber" indicates that it was made during the opening years of the Yüan Dynasty, during the "19th year of the Chih Yüan period," a date corresponding to 1282. The treasure chamber itself contained fragments of colored silk symbolizing the vital organs along with offerings of raw silk, seeds, bits of incense sticks, and semi-precious stones (*cf.* contents of *No. 21,* the Golden Boy). The inscription makes this splendid work a key monument in the history of Chinese wood sculpture, in which verifiable dates are few and far between. It has helped identify as late Sung or early Yüan a whole series of sculptures with similar characteristics, among which the most distinctive are the rectangular shape of the face (when viewed head-on) and the trough-like fold of the drapery between the legs. The peculiar way in which the hair is drawn into a knot before it divides into three separate strands over the shoulders may also be a mannerism limited to this period.

Here the scarves and lavish jewelry so common in Buddhist sculpture, even in examples of roughly the same date, have been reduced to a minimum. The pose still basically follows a classic formula developed during the T'ang Dynasty. The bare chest, the hip thrust slightly to one side, and the arm on the same side bent at the elbow and upraised are all part of this formula. The turn of the head and the position of the left arm, however, give this figure a sense of animation that would never be found in its T'ang prototypes. It is as though the Bodhisattva had stopped in mid movement to take in something that had suddenly caught its attention. Even the drapery, for all its understatement, seems charged with energy and movement when set beside comparable figures from the eighth century.

This superb work stands as proof that Chinese Buddhist sculpture in wood—many authoritative assertions to the contrary notwithstanding—was still flourishing at the end of the thirteenth century.

The front part of the left foot has been broken off and the corresponding part of the right foot, which was also broken off, has been replaced. The left hand may once have held a water jar or perhaps a lotus blossom, a portion of which, now too fragmentary to be identifiable, is still clasped between the fingers. Extensive areas of polychrome remain.

48

18. STANDING LOHAN

Late Yüan or early Ming Dynasty, 14th-15th century
Height: 86.4 cm.
Asian Art Museum of San Francisco, the Avery Brundage Collection

Depictions of the lohans often come extremely close to portraiture.
No. 15 was one example; this is another. Here one's attention is
naturally first drawn to the face, with its prominent forehead, deep
brow, broad nose, and firm lips, but the lohan seems to emanate
strength of character by his stance and very build as well. A sturdy
figure, clad in the garments of a monk, he seems intensely
practical for all the introspective spirituality of his gaze.

He holds his hands up in front of him as though to cradle some
object that has now been lost. Holes in his long, pendant earlobes
suggest that he once wore earrings. The figure is much weathered
and shows signs of extensive decay, yet traces of gesso and
pigments remain.

19. THE MONK PU-TAI
Ming Dynasty, 15th-16th century
Height: 67.3 cm.
Cleveland Museum of Art. Gift of R. Hosomi

This jovial, potbellied figure is the eccentric monk Pu-tai (Hotei, in Japanese). A well-known character in the Ch'an tradition which included the famous pair, Han-shan and Shih-te, and their companion Fêng-kan accompanied by his faithful pet tiger. Whether or not these rather bizarre and eccentric personages ever actually existed is somewhat doubtful. We have little real substantial biographical information that can be positively linked with any members of the group.

Pu-tai is said to have resided in the area around Ssu-ming (present-day Ningpo) in south China during the later Liang Dynasty and to have died in the year 916 or 917 A.D. He was said to have wandered around the countryside begging for food and alms and placing everything he received in a huge hemp-cloth bag which he always carried with him. A bald, unkempt figure, his huge belly exposed, he came to be known as Pu-tai or "Hemp Bag," his cloth sack being one of the distinguishing features by which he is known. However, his big belly is also one of his trademarks, and his name became a metaphor for this feature too. Later he came to be regarded as an avatar of the Buddha Maitreya, and in Japan, where he is known as Hotei, he is worshipped as one of the Seven Gods of Good Fortune *(shichi-fuku-jin)*.

Here we see the smiling monk standing with his arms stretched back above his head and his feet placed firmly on the ground. His fat belly protrudes above an apron-like garment hanging down over his trousers and secured with a sash tied in a neat bow. His legs, which are abnormally short, are set wide apart. The fabric of his trousers cling to his legs in squared-off rectangular depressions that emphasize the block-like appearance of the legs themselves. There is a peculiar stylized symmetry to the figure, noticeable especially in the treatment of the legs and the nearly identical openings between the ends of the dangling sleeves and the monk's midriff. The belly is red, the garments a greenish black.

20. GOLDEN BOY
Late Sung Dynasty (?)
Height: 69.8 cm.
The Metropolitan Museum of Art, New York.
Gift of Mrs. John D. Rockefeller, Jr., 1942

Child attendants of Kuan-yin, such as this "Golden Boy" and his usual companion, Yü Nü, the "Jade Girl," seem to be a purely Chinese invention; they are never found, at any rate, in Japan.

A point by point comparison with *No. 21*, probably a somewhat later version of the same subject, is revealing. The two pieces are quite close in size, yet this one, which is actually shorter, gives a greater impression of height, created, in part, by the fact that the figure itself is more slender but also by the strong, continuous sweep of the garments. This directional energy moving through the garments is one of the more remarkable features of the work. Much of the original red of the robe remains.

The two figures are also quite close in pose, even agreeing in such details as the angle at which the feet point away from one another; but the Seattle figure looks straight ahead while this one gazes up, a difference no doubt dictated by the different heights of the images they were made to accompany.

In spite of all the similarities, the final impression made by the two works is strikingly different. Additional reasons for this will be pointed out in the next entry.

21. GOLDEN BOY (CHILD ATTENDANT OF KUAN-YIN)
Ming Dynasty (1368-1644)
Height: 67.3 cm.
Seattle Art Museum. Eugene Fuller Memorial Collection

Perhaps the biggest difference between this "Golden Boy" and its counterpart from New York is in the treatment of the garments. To be sure, the child itself is chubbier and more baby-like here, but this is a minor difference. The fluttering robe, with its agitated hemline, on the other hand, bears no resemblance whatever to the garment worn by the other child. The relief pattern of clouds and phoenixes enhanced with polychrome and gold leaf contribute to the surface complexity of this robe, which contrasts interestingly with the simple mass of the figure itself. The final effect, however, is perhaps more painterly than sculptural.

A small, rectangular plug in the back covers a treasure chamber hollowed out inside. In 1957, this chamber was opened and a curious inventory of objects removed (see above). The custom of placing charms, offerings, and other items of magical import inside a figure was a common one in China and Japan. Sometimes the contents make it possible to date the figure in question *(cf. No. 17)*, but in this instance the figure was presumably rededicated for a Lamaist temple near Peking some time during the seventeenth or eighteenth century, and the contents are of that date and of Tibetan rather than Chinese origin.

The contents included a bronze mirror, fabric in the shape of various vital organs, charms, seeds, herbs, semi-precious stones, bits of metal, and a metal pendant.

22. GOOSE
Late Sung Dynasty (?)
Height: 66.1 cm.
Mr. and Mrs. James W. Alsdorf, Winnetka, Illinois

It is hard to imagine how this goose would have been used. The goose figures prominently in Chinese folklore and is often depicted in painting, but sculptural representations are rare. A goose-like bird is occasionally found in Esoteric Buddhism, where it appears as the mount of one of the five Kokuzō Bodhisattvas; but this is clearly intended as a humbler creature than that; in fact, it can only represent the familiar domestic fowl of the barnyard.

The anonymous carver was clearly familiar with his subject; yet the work has some of the naivete about it that one associates with folk art. It has been built up from a series of separate pieces, or planks, of wood. The cracks between these pieces can be clearly made out now that most of the gesso has been lost. The plain, almost box-like structure of the body is particularly interesting. The feathers are effectively, if rather summarily, indicated by a series of simple gouge marks.

23. RECLINING HORSE
   Ming Dynasty (1368-1644)
   Height: 20.3 cm.
   Mr. and Mrs. John D. Rockefeller III

   In its size, compactness, and general conformation this lacquered
   wood horse is more than a little reminiscent of the carved jade
   horses of the same period. The solidity of the piece and the firmness
   of the carving add further to this initial impression. The jade
   horses, however, generally show less animation, as one might
   expect in carvings of the more obdurate material. Here the tail
   twitches, the nostrils seem to quiver, and the left hind leg is
   bent at the hoof. The entire piece is covered with lustrous brown
   lacquer with touches of black.

24. PAIR OF LAUGHING CHILDREN

Ch'ing Dynasty, K'ang-hsi Period, 1662-1722
Height: 16.5 cm.
Mr. and Mrs. James W. Alsdorf, Winnetka, Illinois

Paintings of playful children were popular in China already as
early as the twelfth century, and the subject apparently never
lost its charm or disappeared completely from the standard
repertory of figure painting. Sculptures of children are rarer, apart
from figures like the Golden Boy *(Nos. 20 and 21).* On the other
hand, children are frequently depicted in miniature carving, either
alone or in the company of some legendary ancient or immortal.
It is quite possible that these two figures were intended to accompany a third and larger figure. Certainly their upturned faces
and delighted smiles seem to be in response to someone or something above them; and the fact that each child reflects, in mirror
fashion, some of the pose and movement of the other, further
supports the possibility that they were flanking pieces. If so,
judging by the jolly expression on their faces, they could only have
accompanied some jovial figure such as Pu-tai *(No. 19)* or Pêng-tsu,
the Chinese Methuselah.

   The carving is simple and direct with more attention given to
the faces than the garments. The children both have shaven heads
with two tufts of hair at either side. Each figure has lost one of
its hands and some of the fingers from the remaining hand.

5. CABBAGE AND BEETLE

Ch'ing Dynasty, mid 18th century
Height: 13.2 cm.
Cleveland Museum of Art. Sundry Purchase Fund

We have already seen one table piece reminiscent of jade carving,
the Ming Dynasty lacquered horse from the Rockefeller Collection
(No. 23). It seemed to be based on those compact, block-like jade
carvings—typical of the Ming Dynasty—that emphasize the
solidity of the material. This extraordinary piece also seems to
have drawn its inspiration from jade carving, but jade carving,
obviously, of an entirely different kind—the virtuoso carving
favored during the Ch'ing Dynasty. Such details as the cord passing
through the copper "cash" and the perforated rock of the base
seem drawn directly from the repertory of the jade craftsmen
of the period. Even the carver's basic approach to his material,
the way he has let the natural gloss and color of the wood speak
for itself, reinforces the analogy with lapidary work. Quite apart
from such analogies, however, simply in terms of woodcarving, the
work is an impressive *tour-de-force* in its own right. Yet it is
more than a mere craftsman's showpiece; the subject is treated
convincingly, and the hard, shiny beetle is an amusing, true-
to-life touch.

When Buddhism first arrived in Japan around the middle of the sixth century, it was almost certainly not seen as a potential rival to the native cult of Shintō but as an integral part of continental Chinese civilization and a powerful new form of magic that could be used to the advantage of those who mastered it. It was not only Buddhism that the Japanese embraced with growing enthusiasm from the late sixth century on but the entire apparatus of Chinese learning, starting with the written language and including new forms of literary and artistic expression, systems of philosophy, and even Chinese theories of statecraft. The most influential advocate of this new Chinese learning—thus also of Buddhism—was Prince Shōtoku Taishi, who was regent from 593 to 622 A.D. *(See Nos. 41 and 58).* It was he who began the custom of sending periodic embassies to China, a practice that continued until well into the ninth century. Student monks accompanying these embassies often stayed on in China, returning only after many years, laden with mementos of their sojourn and with their knowledge of Buddhism and Chinese learning in general immensely enhanced.

It must be remembered that, prior to this period of contact, Japanese society was relatively primitive. There was no written language and only the most simple agrarian economy and rudimentary forms of government. The impact of Chinese culture on such a society must have been enormous.

The first Buddhist temples were established under official patronage and were not so much centers for the propagation of the faith as arenas for the staging of elaborate rituals designed to ensure the stability of the realm and the well-being of the ruling class. As a result, during the first few centuries of its existence in Japan, the

new religion probably made little headway outside fairly limited circles surrounding the court. Within these circles, however, its wealth and prestige grew to impressive proportions, to the point where, in 794, the capital actually had to be moved from Nara to Heiankyō (present day Kyoto) to isolate the government from the excessive influence of the clerical establishment in the older capital.

It was not until the introduction of Esoteric Buddhism, shortly after 800, that the religion began to exert a wider appeal. Esoteric Buddhism, with its mysterious rituals and awesome pantheon, was capable of stirring the imagination far more powerfully than any of the more intellectual sects that had been introduced earlier. Geographically too, Esoteric Buddhism penetrated into areas of the country remote from the metropolitan centers. It also established links with Shintō, by developing a doctrine according to which the native gods were seen as alternate forms, or avatars, of Buddhist deities. Elaborate lists of correspondences were drawn up, and Shintō shrines were actually set up under the "protection" of specific temples. The first anthropomorphic images of the native gods appeared at this time, obviously as a result of these developments.

Esoteric Buddhism remained a force in Japan long after it had died out in China. Its impact on the arts, at least after the period of its first introduction, is somewhat more difficult to assess. Certainly its complex imagery served as a challenge to the skill of successive generations of artists and continued to feed the Japanese imagination for centuries.

The earliest Japanese Buddhist works in this exhibition *(Nos. 26 and 27)* date from the ninth century and are typical of the so-called Jōgan style, named after the Jōgan era (859-876), when the style was most prevalent. Massive, imposing works, they have a sense of somber dignity and brooding power that never recurs in Japanese sculpture after this time. Within little more than a century, in fact, a totally different style—one in many ways its exact antithesis—had begun to emerge in its place. What had been weighty and emphatic gradually became light and understated. Drapery which had once surged in great swells now subsided into almost imperceptible ripples. Underlying and supporting these changes in taste were changes in technique that made their expression possible. The single block, *ichiboku*, technique was well adapted to the Jōgan style, but the new style needed a more flexible technique, which it found in the so-called *yosegi*, joined block, method of construction which was perfected at this time.

By the mid eleventh century the change in taste was complete. It was a change reflecting, in part, changed social and political conditions but also, in part, the growing influence of a new form of Buddhism, Amidism. The cult of Amitabha, or belief in the Pure Land, became increasingly popular in Japan around the end of the tenth century. It was an undemanding creed, and we have already seen how quickly it superseded other forms of Buddhism in China. In Japan, it gained its first adherents among the nobility, who began to build Amida Halls as testimony to their faith. The most famous of these is the Phoenix Hall of the Byōdō-in in Uji, built in 1052, with its great image of Amida by Jōchō, but they all followed a somewhat similar pattern, the idea being to depict Amida in the glory of his paradise or descending in the company of angels and bodhisattvas to receive the faithful. Many of the works in this exhibition were carved for use in such depictions *(Nos. 28, 30, 31,*

and 40; possibly also No. 32). The sculpture developed for these Amida Halls, reflecting as it does both the extreme refinement of Heian aristocratic taste and the visionary ideals of the Pure Land faith, is probably the most perfect expression of the new eleventh century style.

However, this style too was destined to change within little more than a century and a half. A series of wars and disasters, beginning around 1150, culminated in 1185 with the establishment of the Kamakura Shogunate, an event that spelled the shift of effective political power from the aristocracy surrounding the imperial court to the military caste. At the same time, new, evangelical forms of Buddhism began to appear under the leadership of men like Shinran (1173-1262) who were genuinely concerned with spreading the faith and breaking down the distinctions between clergy and laity. It was a more aggressive age, one more interested in direct action and effectiveness, and the art it produced reflected this new focus. Sculpture became more dynamic and realistic, at times almost baroque. Two sculptors, in particular, are associated with these developments, Unkei and his brother Kaikei, founders of the so-called "Kei" school of sculpture. Though this exhibition includes no sculpture by either of these men, it does include work showing their influence, such as the Standing Amida *(No. 40)* in the style of Kaikei.

Meanwhile, contact with China, which had virtually ceased after the mid ninth century, had resumed, though on an unofficial basis. Once more Japanese student monks braved the hazardous voyage across the Japan Sea on pilgrimages to the ancient centers of Buddhism on the continent. The Ch'an sect was particularly active in China at this time, and it is only natural that some of these monks were attracted to its teachings, which they propagated upon their return home. This marks the first real emergence of Ch'an—or Zen—in Japan, where ultimately it was to have a pervasive influence on nearly every aspect of life. Beginning around 1200 the sect produced a series of remarkable leaders whose strength of character and exacting self-discipline won them the respect—and eventually the patronage—of the shogunate. The Zen interest in portraiture combined with the Kamakura emphasis on realism to produce some of the most powerful sculpture of the period. The Portrait of Hōtō Kokushi *(No. 44)* is a worthy example of the type. The inspiration for portrait sculpture of this sort was found in the painted portraits of their masters—the so-called chinsō portraits—which the Japanese monks brought back from China as mementos of their stay and proof that they had satisfactorily completed their training.

There are those who maintain that no Buddhist sculpture of consequence was produced in Japan after the Kamakura Period. Though it would be difficult to support so blanket an assertion, certainly there was a marked falling off in the inspiration of Buddhist sculpture after that time. The work of Enkū *(No. 61)* is only the exception that proves the rule. The best of later Japanese sculpture drew its inspiration from other quarters.

26. GUARDIAN FIGURE

Heian Period, 9th century
Height: 94.0 cm.
N. V. Hammer, New York

This was one of the four guardian figures, or "Heavenly Kings," that surrounded and protected the principal image on a Buddhist altar. Each of these guardians was associated with one of the four cardinal directions and, when intact and in its original setting, could be identified by its placement and attributes. The aggressive stance and scowling demeanor is standard in these guardians, whose whole purpose is to ward off evil. Originally, the arms in this figure would have brandished a weapon or been raised in menace, and the left foot would have been planted atop a squirming demon. The armor is essentially that of a Chinese military officer of the T'ang Dynasty, its most distinctive feature being the animal-mask buckle, which actually sinks its teeth into the rolled sash girdling the figure's waist. Trousers or pantaloons puff out above tight greaves on both legs, and a thick tail or train hangs down behind.

The figure is carved in the *ichiboku* technique from a single block of wood, with the exception of the left leg from the projecting knee on down. It is not certain whether this piece was originally separate or whether it is a later replacement. (Interestingly enough, a related figure, probably from the same set, in the Asian Art Museum of San Francisco, has a projecting leg treated in the same way.) The front half of the right foot is definitely a later replacement, as is the very back of the topknot.

The bulkiness and massiveness of this figure is typical of the Jōgan style which flourished during the mid ninth century. Surface detail, however, is minimal, as though the sculptor was reluctant to cut too deeply into the central trunk of the wood, and it ends up looking somewhat stolid by comparison with the next piece (also from the same period) with its bolder carving.

27. JIZŌ BODHISATTVA

Heian Period, ca. 900
Height: 107.0 cm.
The Art Museum, Princeton University

This powerfully carved and rather austere figure clad in a simple monk's robe represents the popular Bodhisattva Jizō, one of the most widely worshipped deities in Japanese Buddhism. Known as Kshitegarbha in Sanskrit, meaning the "matrix of the Earth," he is usually represented in the guise of a Buddhist monk, wearing none of the elaborate scarves or jewelry usually associated with bodhisattvas.

The cult of Jizō reached Japan during the mid eighth century, and even today statues of him are often seen along country roads and streets and near cemeteries. He is worshipped as the helper of all in trouble, especially the weak or suffering, and is prayed to for his blessings over expectant mothers, young children, travellers, soldiers on the battlefield, and those doomed to an existence in Hell.

Jizō is most often seen standing on a lotus flower and carrying a long pilgrim's staff, or *shakujō*, in his right hand and a burning jewel *(Nyoi-shu)* in his left. The jewel, which was supposed to be capable of responding to all wishes and illuminating the darkness of Hell, is also an attribute of Nyoirin Kannon *(No. 45)*.

This powerful figure is without doubt one of the finest examples of ninth century Japanese sculpture in this country. Of course, a standing or walking figure is inherently more compatible with the *ichiboku* process than a more violent or active figure such as one of the Heavenly Kings; yet this sculpture does more than merely comply with the limitations of this process, it actually turns these limitations to advantage. The massiveness and bulk of the piece and the heavy, regularly repeated folds give it an extraordinary authority and sense of purposiveness.

Long cracks extend from the head down through the torso, and there has been considerable decay at the very bottom. The right foot is missing, as is the left hand, which was the only part of the figure carved from a separate piece of wood. The hand would have held the jewel mentioned earlier as being one of the attributes of Jizō.

28. AMIDA NYORAI

Late Heian Period, 12th century
Height: 91.4 cm.
Asian Art Museum of San Francisco,
the Avery Brundage Collection

Seated cross-legged in the lotus posture, hands joined in the *mudra*
of contemplation and eyes all but closed, this is a more aloof
image of Amida than the one developed later by Kaikei *(cf. No. 40).*
Here the prototype is the famous sculpture by Jōchō, in the
Byōdō-in, dated 1053. Here, as there, what one is offered is a
vision, a vision of Amida enthroned in his paradise. In the Byōdō-in,
that vision is enhanced by the setting, a dazzling halo behind the
image, a canopy overhead, and a heavenly orchestra in relief on
the walls. We must imagine that this figure once enjoyed a similar
setting. The elaborate, seven-layered lotus pedestal is all that
now remains of it.

The image itself reflects the ideals of Heian aristocratic taste,
a taste of exquisite refinement and understatement. There is none
of the massiveness and strength of earlier images. The robes seem
lightweight and tend to cling to the body, forming only the
shallowest of folds. The face registers no emotion.

29. APSARAS

Heian Period, second half of the 11th century
Height: 85.1 cm.
Museum of Fine Arts, Boston

This plump-faced figure, daintily manipulating a pair of clappers, is an *apsaras*, a heavenly nymph or angelic musician, borne aloft on a scroll shaped cloud that merges with the angel's fluttering, upswept skirt. Reputed to have come from the halo of an Amida image at the Kōfuku-ji in Nara, it clearly was intended as part of a larger ensemble, whether affixed to a halo or not. Comparable figures are attached to the wall behind the great Seated Amida at the Byōdō-in. This figure seems softer and more rounded than those, however, and the scarves, skirts, and limbs seem to merge more completely. There is also less surface detail. The Byōdō-in figures date from the mid eleventh century; this one is probably a generation later.

Eleventh century images of Amida were frequently surrounded by smaller figures of angels and bodhisattvas, representing the host of heavenly attendants who accompany Amida when he descends to receive a dying believer into paradise.

30. APSARAS, FLYING ATTENDANT OF AMIDA

Heian Period, 11th century
Height: 94.0 cm.
Seattle Art Museum. Eugene Fuller Memorial Collection

This *apsaras*, which is also said to have come from the halo of a Buddha image (though not necessarily an image of Amida), provides some interesting points of comparison with *No. 29*. The scarves, which are more complete, billow up with extraordinary flame-like energy, and the double cloud underneath seems much more rumpled and complex than the comparable form in *No. 29*. Everything about the earlier piece seems softer, more muted, more immediately sensuous. The figure itself is more voluptuous, its pose more supple. In fact, by comparison, there is something very flat and straightforward about this figure, and its legs are spread apart in a relatively ungainly fashion. The arms have been broken off at the elbows, so it is impossible to say whether it might have held a musical instrument or not.

There is another, very similar *apsaras*, of about the same size but facing in the opposite direction, at the Honolulu Academy of Arts. It was acquired from the same source and is said to have come from the same halo.

31. SEATED MUSICIAN (SHŌ PLAYER)

Heian Period, *ca.* 1100
Height: 26.0 cm.
The St. Louis Art Museum. W. K. Bixby Oriental Art Trust Fund

Much has been written about the exquisite refinement of Japanese
court taste during the Heian Period, a refinement that touched
every aspect of aristocratic life during the eleventh century. The
Buddhist arts too were transformed by this pervasive sensibility,
and images of extraordinary grace and elegance were produced as a
result. Among them was this tiny musician, its hands delicately
poised to hold a now vanished musical instrument, probably an
ancient reed instrument known as a *shō*. The figure must have
formed part of a celestial orchestra accompanying an image of
Amida Nyorai (though no actual such ensemble is known to exist).
It is probably most comparable to some of the relief figures of
musicians on the walls of the Byōdō-in, though it is less than
half the size of those and is carved with less detail. Somehow,
its diminutive size and very isolation emphasize the detached,
dream-like quality that makes this gentle figure so typical of
its period.

32. APSARAS
Late Kamakura Period, early 14th century
Height: 39.4 cm.
Asian Art Museum of San Francisco,
the Avery Brundage Collection

Though later in date and more fragmentary than *Nos. 29 and 30*,
this figure too is thought to have been part of a halo. If so, its
position in the halo relative to the Buddha image itself is clearly
indicated by the turn of its body and the downward direction of
its gaze: it would be somewhat above and to the left of that image.
There is, of course, no way of knowing how many other *apsaras*
would have been attached to the halo. There is also no way of
knowing what scarves might have surrounded this figure or
whether or not it was seated on a cloud. The band of drapery
circling the upper arm may well have been part of a scarf swirling
out behind it as in *No. 30*. A series of small holes above the forehead suggest that some ornament might have been attached at
that point. The object in the *apsaras'* hand is a lotus bud. The piece
has been severely charred at the bottom and has suffered considerable damage otherwise. As a result, it is rather difficult to compare
it stylistically with *Nos. 29 and 30*. It is, however, somewhat
harder than *No. 29*, which, as was pointed out earlier, seems
modeled with unusual fluency.

33. FUDŌ MYŌ-Ō

Late Heian or early Kamakura Period,
late 12th-early 13th century
Height: 48.9 cm.
Mr. and Mrs. John D. Rockefeller, III

Although the Godai Myō-ō, the Five Great Kings of Light, are of Indian origin, they are never seen as a group in India and appear to have first been conceived and represented as a group of five in China during the eighth century.

In Japan, where the cult of the five Myō-ō has been particularly prevalent, Fudō Myō-ō (Acala, in Sanskrit) has found the greatest recognition, and special devotion to him has been widespread. Emanations of Dainichi Nyorai (Mahāvairocana), the Myō-ō are ferocious and wrathful in appearance but compassionate and benevolent in nature and function as protectors of the faith and subjugators of evil forces.

Fudō, the "Immovable or Unshakable," first appears as a messenger and servant of the Buddha and it is only in the Dainichi-kyō (Vairocana sutra), the primary scripture for Esoteric Buddhism, that he is described in greater iconographic detail as a Myō-ō, or "King of Light." In the arrangement of the five Myō-ō within Esoteric temples, Fudō occupies the central position, with the other four placed at the four cardinal directions (Kongō Yasha in the North, Daiitoku in the South, Gōsanze in the East, and Gundari in the West) giving visual representation to the Esoteric cosmos with Dainichi at the center, from whom all things emanate

The most renowned example in sculpture of this type of mandala, or diagrammatic scheme of the universe, is found in the lecture hall of Tōji, built in 794 A.D., in Kyōto. Dating to *ca.* 839 A.D., these sculptures in wood mark one of the supreme achievements in Esoteric Buddhist art.

In contrast to the powerful and muscular physiques of the Niō, or Benevolent Kings, also subjugators of evil forces and guardians of the faith, the body of Fudō Myō-ō seems relatively child-like with undeveloped muscles and softly modeled limbs.

Here, Fudō sits with one leg pendant, an iconographical feature not particularly common in sculptures of this deity (where he is usually shown sitting cross-legged) but one often found in paintings.

He is usually shown with two attributes: in his right hand, a sword to cut down the guilty; and in his left, a lasso to arrest the evil and bring them to true knowledge. Here both attributes are missing. Although we find that in most Japanese examples Fudō is seen with both eyes wide open and bulging, here he is depicted in accordance with the descriptions given in the sūtras, with one eye tightly closed. His hair is arranged in snail-like curls and the prescribed plait of hair which usually hangs down to the left of the face is missing.

TWO SHŌ KANNON

34. Late Heian Period, 12th century
   Height: 47.0 cm.
   The Mary and Jackson Burke Foundation, New York City

35. Late Heian Period, 12th century
   Height: 48.2 cm.
   The Brooklyn Museum

These fragile, cypress-wood images of Kannon are thought to
have come from a group of a thousand such sculptures once
enshrined on a large altar or special hall within the precincts of the
Kōfuku-ji in Nara. There is no historical record of this, but large
numbers of these images were sold by the temple in the late 19th
century, and numerous examples are known to exist in private
collections in both this country and Japan. For objects that must
have been virtually mass-produced, there is considerable variation
in gesture and costume from figure to figure and the images are
uniformly graceful and delicate. The poise and hint of contrapposto
in *No. 34* is particularly charming. The fragile scarf in *No. 35* is
relatively rare in these figures. Originally both figures would have
been covered with gesso and gold paint; now only traces of the
gesso remain.

   At least several *Sentai-dō*, "Halls of a Thousand Images," were
built in Japan in the 12th century. The idea behind these was one
that appears frequently in Mayāhāna Buddhism, the idea that merit
can be accumulated through the repetition of a pious deed.

36. GUARDIAN FIGURE
Attributed to Jōga, *ca.* 1200
Height: 73.7 cm. (including base)
Minneapolis Museum of Arts

This amusing figure, pursing his lips as though struggling to contain his impish wrath, is one of the Twelve Divine Generals who guard Yakushi Nyorai, the Buddha of Healing. He wears the armor of a Chinese officer of the T'ang Dynasty and in this respect (as well as others) resembles the Four Heavenly Kings (see *No. 26*), as one of whom he might have been taken were it not for the little animal poking its head from his curious, bag-like cap. From the late Heian Period on, the Generals, being twelve in number, came to be associated with the twelve animals of the Eastern Zodiac. The animal in this instance is difficult to identify, though it may well be a dog.

In all likelihood this little figure originally held a weapon (or weapons) in his clenched hands. It is difficult to say to what extent this might have altered the impression he makes. As it is, his ferocity seems rather ineffectual, like the tantrums of a gnome.

He strikes a rather rigid pose by comparison with other guardian figures of the period, which, with their fluttering sleeves and dramatic gestures, seem much more animated. There is even something a little stubby, almost dwarfish, about him. Yet one must remember that, originally, he would have been only one of an ensemble of twelve figures, each striking a different posture, bristling around a central image of Yakushi Nyorai.

The Brooklyn Museum has a guardian figure (see right) that may very well be from this same set. It is about the same size, stands on a similar pedestal, and has some of the same compact stubbiness. The animal is missing from his cap but has clearly been lost. In both figures, the eyes are carved rather than set in. Interestingly, both figures have been attributed to Jōga, a sculptor principally known for his association with Jōkei (of the Kei School) in work done for the Kōfuku-ji, Nara, around 1200. The Minneapolis figure is said to bear an inscription (inside?) ascribing it to Jōga.

37. TORSO OF GUARDIAN KING
Kamakura Period (1185-1333)
Height: 99.7 cm.
Seattle Art Museum

Such shell-like torsos, roughly hollowed out behind, are typical of an early transitional stage in the development of the *yosegi*, or joined wood, technique. The heads, trunks, and legs of earlier figures, such as *No. 26*, were usually carved from a single block of wood, and the sculpture, as a result, usually seemed more massive. Here the limbs, head, and back were all carved separately and carefully fitted together afterwards. Note the exposed tool marks and mortises and the large notch cut to receive the bulk of the left thigh. The back would have been thinner, and less deeply carved.

A comparison with *No. 26* is instructive. Both pieces wear similar, very simple armor with lion masks at their belts, and both pieces are carved in relatively shallow relief (with the exception of the deep parallel folds in the sash falling over the loins in this example). Here there is a slight twist to the body, however, and the torso is much less stocky. No polychrome remains on either piece.

38. RAMBA AND BIRAMBA

Kamakura Period (1185-1333)
Height: Biramba, 42 cm.; Ramba, 43.8 cm.
Seattle Art Museum

These two demon-like creatures with menacing facial expressions often flank the earth-goddess Jiten, forming with her a base support for representations of Tobatsu Bishamonten, a variant form of the guardian King of the North, Bishamonten (or Tamonten).

Here, dwarfed in their proportions, their hands clasped at their chests, and in squatting positions, they seem to bear an affinity to the set of goblin-like figures attendant on the image of En no Gyōja (the seventh century mountain hermit and founder of the Shugendō sect) in the Sainan-in, Taimadera, Nara. Although they are not always included when Jiten appears with Tobatsu Bishamonten, their connection with her and with En no Gyōja and the fact that they do not appear among the figures of the Buddhist pantheon of the continent, suggest a Shintō origin.

There is something almost amusing about these squat little figures with their scowling expressions, bulging eyes, and knit brows. They have no necks—their heads are placed directly on their shoulders—but they do have prominent collar bones. They are naked from the waist up and wear only a brief garment on the lower part of their bodies. Particularly prominent are the round, bulging muscles on the legs and arms. The rough chiseling is typical of the so-called *natabori* technique, which seems to have been confined to Northern Japan.

Made in the solid block, *ichiboku*, technique, the figures have cracked in several places and have been repaired. Traces of pigment still exist, especially on areas that have been better protected, such as on the back and under the arms.

39. NIŌ (KONGŌ-RIKISHI)
Kamakura Period, 13th century
Height: Misshaku Kongō—76.2 cm.
Naraen Kongō—76.8 cm.
The Cleveland Museum of Art.
Purchase, Andrew R. and Martha Holden Jennings Fund

These two colossal heads represent Misshaku Kongō, with his open mouth and bared teeth, and Naraen Kongō, with his mouth closed in a fierce grimace. Signifying respectively overt power and latent might, these two Niō, or "Benevolent Kings," were guardians of temple precincts, placed at the temple gate to ward off danger and evil forces from the vicinity.

Niō are usually represented as powerful figures with exaggerated muscle structure and bulging veins. They were an especially popular subject during the Kamakura Period when the baroque taste of the time was attracted to the dramatic possibilities offered by their varied and complex bodily movements, powerful and often exaggerated muscle and bone structure, and intense, frightful facial expressions. The best-known pair of Niō carved then still stand today at the Nandaimon (South Main Gate) of the Tōdai-ji, Nara. They are of enormous size, measuring 834 and 842 cm., and were the joint work of Unkei and Kaikei, the two most important leaders of the Kei school.

Niō are most commonly seen either with their heads entirely shaven or, as here, with a neatly tied chignon left at the top. Their menacing countenances, bulging eyes, knitted brows, and scowling expressions clearly indicate their function as protectors of the faith and of the temple complex. Note the swollen veins of the temples.

Considering that these heads alone measure thirty inches, the complete figures must have been of considerable height. One can only imagine the impression they must have made.

40. STANDING AMIDA

Kamakura Period, late 12th-early 13th century
Height: 82.6 cm.
The St. Louis Art Museum

Toward the end of the Heian Period a new image of Amida emerged, a gentle, compassionate image emphasizing the promise of salvation he offered those who believed in him. It is this aspect of the deity that is graphically represented in the so-called *raigō* paintings, which depict a radiant Amida, accompanied by angels and bodhisattvas, descending to earth to receive the faithful. Sculptures like this, which became popular at the same time, can be thought of as three-dimensional representations of the same concept. They too show Amida gazing down upon the worshipper, his left hand palm outward and his right hand upraised in a gesture of welcome. It is a beautiful and moving image and one that has been cherished by Japanese Buddhists for centuries. Though sculptures with many of the same iconographic features had existed earlier, it was not until the opening years of the Kamakura Period, around 1200, that this image achieved its classic formulation. The sculptor credited with this development is Kaikei, who, together with his brother Unkei, was a major force behind the revitalization of Japanese sculpture that took place at this time. Kaikei was a devout Amidist, and the style he perfected—the so-called An-ami style—was imbued with all the gentle idealism that one associates with that faith.

This sculpture was formerly attributed to Kaikei but is probably the work of a follower of a generation or so later. The face is more youthful and its expression sweeter than in any of the recognized sculptures by Kaikei. In Kaikei's work, the gentleness and lyricism still seem balanced by a certain gravity. Here that gravity has all but disappeared. There are more folds to the drapery, and the robes, as a consequence, almost seem to flutter. There is an extraordinary daintiness to the hands. For all this, the work still is remarkably faithful to Kaikei's vision and serves as a noble representative of one of the high-points of Japanese Buddhist sculpture.

41. SHŌTOKU TAISHI AT AGE SIXTEEN
Kamakura Period, 1185-1333
Height: 61.6 cm.
Seattle Art Museum. Eugene Fuller Memorial Collection

Shōtoku Taishi (574-622), revered as Japan's foremost patron of Buddhism during the critical years of its first introduction, was a scion of the Imperial family and Regent from 593 until his death. His actual historical accomplishments are difficult to separate from the many legends about him that began to spring up already in the seventh century. He became the subject of innumerable paintings and sculptures, particularly from the late Heian Period on, by which time he was considered, by some sects, a re-incarnation of Shakyamuni or the Bodhisattva Kannon. Each of the new sects of the Kamakura Period attempted to demonstrate some link with the prince, in the process adding further to the legends surrounding him.

Here he is shown as a boy of sixteen, taking part in rites for the recovery of his father, the ailing Emperor Yōmei. Images of Shōtoku Taishi usually take one of three forms: as a boy of sixteen, as here; as a two year old child chanting the *nembutsu;* or as Regent issuing a proclamation concerning court ranks. Of the three, this is probably the most frequently depicted. Interestingly enough, most of the better known images of this type in Japan show him wearing a priest's robe, or *kesa*, and seem to be more formal and imposing. By contrast, there is something very appealing

and human about him as shown here. He still seems a little stocky and child-like as he hunches forward, a look of genuine concern on his face. His features resemble those of the earliest extant sculpture of Shōtoku Taishi, a seated figure of 1069 at Hōryūji, a temple closely associated with the prince, who may, in fact, have founded it. That figure, according to temple tradition, represents the prince at age seven. Perhaps some of the child-like features of this figure might derive from the artist's familiarity with that earlier work. This version also differs from other representations in the way the hair is shown, hanging down in two loose pigtails rather than gathered up in buns or coiled at either side.

The face is much worn, especially the forehead, nose, and chin, where the grain of the wood is very apparent. On the other hand, the floral pattern on the robe, painted in gold, white, reddish orange, and green, is relatively well preserved, particularly in less exposed areas, such as under the sleeves. Note the low-slung belt, which wraps around and tucks under itself behind. The curious double sleeves are a common feature of these images.

The censer, which is carved separately, may be a later replace-ment. The same may be true of the hands.

42. TENDAI PATRIARCH
Kamakura Period, *ca.* 1200
Height: 36.8 cm.
Minneapolis Museum of Arts

There is a delicacy to this little figure that is difficult to reconcile with the bold economy with which it is carved. The head, gently tilted to one side, and the hands, gesturing as though to expound the Law, have been observed with particular sensitivity; the robes, on the other hand, are rendered with a minimum of detail, the few folds cut surprisingly deep, even for a work carved, as this was, from a single block. The use of the *ichiboku* technique in a piece of this date might, under some circumstances, be considered a mark of provincial origin, yet little else about the work would suggest such a conclusion. On the other hand, it is relatively conservative for a work of the 13th century, particularly if it was intended as a portrait. Portraits of the Kamakura Period are generally much less idealized. Some, such as the portrait of Hōtō Kokushi *(No. 44)* are almost startling realistic. This little figure has been identified as a "Tendai Patriarch," but on what basis is unknown. It does bear a certain resemblance to sculptures of the mid ninth century Tendai priest Enchin, also known as Chishō Daishi.

The parallel diagonal folds cutting across the figure's midriff may represent a *kesa* like the one worn by Hōtō Kokushi; but if so, the carving is even more minimal than indicated.

43. STANDING PRIEST
Kamakura Period (1185-1333)
Height: 24.7 cm.
The University of Michigan Museum of Art, Ann Arbor, Michigan.
James Marshall Plumer Memorial Collection

No matter how small or unpretentious an object is, it is still apt to
reflect the same stylistic changes seen in larger, more "important"
work. This is certainly true of this modest little figure, which could
only have been made during the Kamakura Period. The sculptor
has made no effort to idealize his subject, who stares out at us
with one foot upraised, resting on some support, as though
he were casually posing for his portrait. The almost endearingly
homely face has been treated with great frankness; and there is
a certain contrast between the careful modeling it has received and
the much more simplified carving of the body, which retains
some of the columnar quality found in earlier work.

44. HŌTŌ KOKUSHI

Kamakura Period, *ca.* 1286
Height: 91.4 cm.
Cleveland Museum of Art. Purchase, Leonard C. Hanna, Jr. Bequest

This superb example of Zen *chinsō* sculpture depicts the priest Muhon Kakushin (1207-1298) as an old man absorbed in meditation. Every detail of the priest's physiognomy—large ears, sunken cheeks, small mouth—is observed with the directness and unflinching realism that one associates with the best of Zen portraiture. Curiously, such directness is never demeaning to its subject. Invariably, as here, the dignity and strength of personality of those portrayed shine through. One is convinced that they are, as their followers believed, men who have realized their essential Buddha nature and become "Transmitters of the Law." We can see that Kakushin was a man of considerable consequence. A revered teacher as well, and the founder of a school of Zen that gained considerable success in the provinces, he was awarded the posthumous title of Hōtō Kokushi (*Kokushi* means "National Teacher," and Hōtō means "Lamp of the Law").

There are two other sculptures of the priest Kakushin, both in Japan. One, showing him as a younger man, was found to contain material dating it to 1275; the other, in which he seems to be about the same age as here, is dated 1286. Both sculptures obviously could have been made from life. It is uncertain whether this one was or not. It came from the *Myōshin-ji* in Wakayama Prefecture, not far from Kakushin's principal temple, the Kōkoku-ji,

where the image of 1286 is still enshrined.

For all its realism, this sculpture follows certain well established conventions. The severe formality, the way the robes are spread out to give bulk and authority to an image which might otherwise seem too slight, the emphasis on frontality—even the precise placement of the shoes—are features common to all *chinsō* portraits. There is only one respect in which this sculpture departs from tradition—the fact that the priest is seated on a simple bench instead of the usual high-backed chair.

The priest is seated in the lotus posture, the standard posture of Zen meditation, his legs drawn up and crossed under him—hence the empty shoes, hence also the empty robes which spread out over the front of the bench.

Surface wear and damage have exposed the basic structure of this piece, revealing the separate rectangular blocks from which it was joined. From the late Heian Period on, almost all Japanese sculpture was made in this way, using the so-called *yosegi* technique; yet, viewing a finished piece, one is seldom aware of the systematic construction underlying it. Even here the separate blocks are so completely transformed as they take their place in the total work that one readily overlooks them.

45. NYOIRIN KANNON
Late Kamakura Period, late 13th-early 14th century
Height: 49.5 cm.
Mr. and Mrs. John D. Rockefeller III

Probably no other figure in the Buddhist pantheon appears in a greater variety of forms than Avalokitesvara, the Bodhisattva of Compassion, known in Japan as Kannon, in China as Kuan-yin. Certainly some of the most awesome icons in all of Mahāyāna Buddhism are those depicting this Bodhisattva in one or another of its esoteric manifestations, with many heads or arms. Among these the most extravagant is undoubtedly the Thousand-armed Kannon, but other forms too are capable of making a powerful appeal to the imagination. The Eleven-headed Kuan-yin (No. 9) discussed earlier is one of these. The six-armed Nyoirin Kannon, shown here, is another.

According to esoteric teachings, Nyoirin Kannon presided over the highest of the Six Levels of Existence (rokudō), that of the devas. Normally he is shown holding four emblems, or attributes: the wheel of the law, a flaming jewel, a lotus flower, and a rosary. The name, *nyoirin*, derives from the Japanese words for two of these, *nyoishu*, the jewel, and *hōrin*, the wheel. These attributes, though now missing, would originally have been held

by this figure too, the wheel in the upraised outer left hand, the jewel in the middle right hand.

The earliest and most famous representation of Nyoirin Kannon in Japan is the image enshrined in the Golden Hall of Kanshin-ji, not far from Osaka. Dating from the mid ninth century, it has a formal, hieratic quality that is missing in this figure made over four centuries later. Here the eyes are almost completely closed and the head, inclined gently to one side, rests drowsily against the upper right hand. In comparison with the Kanshin-ji image (with which it is virtually identical in iconography), everything about this figure seems more rounded, more fluent, less stiff and withdrawn. The drapery is more elaborate and playful and even the hair is wavier. The result is an image of considerable grace but lacking the mysterious power that seems to emanate from the Kanshin-ji image. The change is analogous to what took place in Chinese Buddhist sculpture during the same period. There too, as we have seen, the evolution was towards increased humanization and accessibility.

46. DRAGON-HEAD POLE TOP
Late Heian or early Kamakura Period, 12th century
Height: 30.5 cm.
Seattle Art Museum. Eugene Fuller Memorial Collection.

Mention was made earlier of the gorgeous settings provided for
the icons arrayed in the Golden Halls of the great temples. There
was a lavish—at times even theatrical—side to Buddhism which
was even more apparent, perhaps, during those important
ceremonial occasions when massed priests in dazzling robes,
carrying censers and other ritual implements and intoning sūtras,
moved in procession from building to building within the temple
grounds. Among the paraphernalia used on these occasions were
long poles from which banners or emblems were suspended. This
piece and the next *(No. 48)* were the ornamental tops of such poles.

   This is probably the earlier of the two pieces; certainly it seems
the more conservative. Richer, more decorative, less theatrical
and more purely ceremonial, the creature itself seems more
serpentine, the forms more sinuous and undulating. Only traces
of pigment remain, on the eyes and between the scales on the
underside of the neck. Horns may have been attached to the head
at one time; there are two holes which might have served for that
purpose. The forehead is a separate block of wood; the head and
neck are otherwise all of one piece. Note that the scales are *carved*
rather than painted as in *No. 47.*

94

47. DRAGON'S HEAD
   Kamakura Period (1185-1333)
   Height: 28.2 cm.
   The University of Michigan Museum of Art, Ann Arbor, Michigan.
   Margaret Watson Parker Art Collection

There is something theatrical, almost make-believe, about the
rumpled snout, full complement of teeth, and scaly chin beard of
this later dragon head. It has been dated to the Kamakura Period,
which is certainly the earliest it could have been carved. The
theatrical approach and the attention given to realistic details
like the snout and teeth would rule out anything earlier.

   The horn, which is carved from a separate piece of wood, seems
to be original, though damaged and somewhat cut down where
it fits into the head. The polychrome, extensive areas of which
remain, also seems to be original. The head is said to have come
from the Kōfuku-ji in Nara.

48. KEMAN (ALTAR PENDANT)
Kamakura Period (1185-1333)
Height: 30.5 cm.
Seattle Art Museum. Thomas D. Stimson Memorial Collection

Keman were pendants hung from horizontal beams near the altars
of Buddhist temples. Originally, decorative streamers hung from
the metal rings at the bottom of these pendants.

Keman had their origin in the wreaths or garlands of fresh
flowers used in Indian temples and, probably because of this,
always include depictions of a knotted cord and flowers in their
design. Occasionally mythological birds or, as here, an *apsaras* are
included as well. Here the *apsaras*, its long scarves floating like
streamers among the flowers, vigorously shakes two percussion
instruments as it lifts up its feet in dance.

Most extant *keman* are of metal. This one, which is of wood,
is quite rare. It is in a remarkable state of preservation, with much
of the polychrome still intact. *Kirikane*, cut gold leaf, has been used
in addition to the polychrome in the robes of the *apsaras*.

49. RAKAN

Edo Period, *ca.* 1690-95
Height: 86.7 cm.
Private collection, anonymous

This is one of a group of over 500 rakan carved during the 1690's for the Edo temple Rakan-ji by the Zen monk Shōun Genkei. Such huge assemblages of figures were not uncommon in the history of Far Eastern Buddhism, in which a fascination with numbers has always been evident. In their original setting, in a vast hall built expressly to house them, the rakan were disposed in tiers on either side of a large central image of Shakyamuni. An illustrated guidebook of 1836 shows this central image seated atop a simulated mountain, indicating that the entire ensemble (which also included several attendant bodhisattvas) was intended to represent Shakyamuni on Vulture Peak expounding the Law to his assembled followers. That original arrangement no longer exists. The hall was destroyed by fire during the late nineteenth century, and the temple was rebuilt on a much smaller scale. Even though all but some ninety of the original group remain, the effect that they create in their present setting is much less impressive. Of the ninety odd pieces that are missing, some were lost in the fire, some have simply deteriorated beyond repair, and some were sold. Several of those sold found their way to this country and are in well-known public collections. The Seattle Art Museum has three, and others are at the Metropolitan Museum of Art, The Detroit Institute of Arts, and the William Rockhill Nelson Gallery-Atkins Museum, Kansas City.

This particular rakan is a well-fleshed figure of considerable dignity and composure. Seated in rapt attention, absorbed inwardly, his gaze is unseeing, but certainly nothing about him—unless, perhaps, the oddly enlarged earlobes—would indicate that he is anything other than an ordinary monk. In this respect this sculpture is very different from many depictions of rakan (even others from this same group), which exaggerate the grotesque features of their subjects.

We have already seen something of the school of portraiture that flourished under Zen patronage *(No. 44)*. An integral part of the Zen tradition is respect for exaggerated marks of character, for whatever is strongly individual. The rakan, with all their eccentricities, were ideal subjects for the Zen artist.

The raised floral pattern on the hem, which contrasts strikingly with the smooth surface of the sculpture otherwise, is a feature of all the figures from Rakan-ji.

Shintō is the native religion of Japan. The word *shintō* means "Way of the Gods," but these gods, or *kami* as they are known in Japanese, are only sometimes conceived in anthropomorphic terms; more often they are thought of as unseen presences, or simply the divinity in things, and as such represent spiritual energies so multitudinous and pervasive as to defy easy systematization. Whatever inspired awe in nature—a river with its powerful current and mysterious eddies, an ancient tree, or a high mountain—could become the object of veneration. The dead, whose influence was felt to continue among the living, were also numbered among the *kami*; and the ancestors of the principal clans—most notably the Imperial, or Yamato, clan—were given positions of honor in the Shintō pantheon.

In a sense, Shintō is less an organized religion than a loosely defined set of disparate beliefs. There is no developed philosophy to tie these beliefs together; they find their unity, rather, in certain shared attitudes and predilections. One of these is a sense of closeness to nature. Even the most august Shintō ritual, with its tremendous emphasis on decorum, is apt to take place in a simple thatched shrine in a dense woods. Much of what we consider typical of Japanese taste—the preference for natural materials such as straw, unfinished wood, or clay—is essentially Shintō in inspiration. Another trait common to Shintō observance is an almost puritanical reluctance to represent or describe the *kami* themselves. It was only relatively late, and then only under strong Buddhist influence, that any effort was made to depict the gods. Many shrines, even now, manage without images altogether; a mirror,

sword, or other cryptic emblem sufficing to symbolize the deity's presence instead. In either case, the object of veneration is rarely, if ever, displayed. Worship takes place outside the shrine; the image or symbol is treasured within, intentionally hidden from view. Nothing could be further from Buddhist usage, where the imagery is calculated to inspire the viewer directly.

Shintō imagery seems simple indeed, almost skimpy in fact, compared with the bewildering complexity of Buddhist iconography. There is a uniformity, an anonymity, to the anthropomorphic figures that makes it impossible to distinguish them one from another on the basis of their attributes. Decorous images clad in court robes, their faces are devoid of emotion. The little goddess included here *(No. 50)* is typical of a whole class of similar figures from which it can be distinguished only in terms of size and style.

The fact that such figures invariably wear court dress points up another feature of institutionalized Shintō, its relationship with the Emperor, who, as a direct earthly descendent of the Sun Goddess, was at once divine ruler and priest king. The ritual and trappings of Shintō reflect this relationship in numerous other ways as well.

Although, as mentioned earlier, Shintō sculpture only arose as the result of Buddhist influence, it soon developed distinctive characteristics of its own. One of these was a preference for the single-block, or *ichiboku*, technique that continued long after that process had been abandoned by Buddhist sculptors. It was as though the Shintō sculptor was hesitant to tamper with the basic nature of the wood. This is particularly apparent in the anthropomorphic figures; in the *koma-inu* and fox guardians, other influences are at work.

50. SHINTŌ GODDESS

Heian Period, *ca.* 9th-10th century
Height: 20.3 cm.
The St. Louis Art Museum. W. K. Bixby Oriental Art Trust Fund

Shintō sculpture abounds in images similar to this one in which
there is little, if anything, in the way of iconography to help
determine the deity represented. Whether male or female, invariably
they wear court dress and are kneeling or seated with hands
joined in front of them. There is an anonymous, conservative
quality to such images that has no counterpart in Buddhist
sculpture with its proliferation of forms.

With her unusually round face, downcast eyes, broad nose,
and fleshy lips, this little figure belongs to a facial type the best
known representative of which is an image of a female deity
belonging to the Ozu Shrine in Shiga Prefecture. That image is
generally dated to the second half of the tenth century.

Here the carving of the face, though somewhat blurred with
age, seems unusually sensitive, particularly for so small a figure.
The face was once covered with *gofun*, traces of which remain.
There are also traces of color and cut gold leaf on the costume.

One particular feature of this figure needs additional comment.
It is the squared off section below the sleeves and above and
between the projecting knees. It seems to represent, in mannered
form, something seen in many of these figures, where the hands
are joined, unseen, under enormously enlarged, muff-like sleeves.
The triangular, petal-shaped form probably represents part of
the skirt thrown over the joined sleeve.

51. SHINTŌ DEITY

Kamakura Period, 12th-13th century
Height: 112.3 cm.
Honolulu Academy of Fine Arts

It is one of the peculiarities of Shintō sculpture that it depicts the
gods as though they were ordinary mortals. As far as any outward
sign is concerned, this could be a simple courtier, an attendant
to some prince. Certainly the costume, the tall peaked cap *(eboshi)*
and baggy pantaloons *(hakama)*, is that of the court; and there is
something about the figure's bearing, as he grasps his pantaloons
with one hand and raises his other hand to his cap as though
making a salute, that seems more appropriate to a retainer.

The sculpture is carved from a single plank of wood in a highly
stylized, simplified fashion. It should be pointed out that Japanese
court dress lends itself to this sort of treatment, since it is very
simply cut from rectangular lengths of fabric with no fitting or
tapering. There is a strong columnar character to this piece, which
is emphasized in the back, where the tunic is given a long tail
that descends all the way to the base. In some respects this tail
resembles a flat pilaster from which the figure projects.

52. PAIR OF KOMA-INU
   Late Kamakura or early Nambokuchō Period, 14th century
   Height: 34.3 cm.
   Mr. and Mrs. John D. Rockefeller III

   Koma-inu, creatures closely resembling lions or Pekinese dogs, are
   usually found in pairs at the entrance or gateway of a Shintō
   shrine or shrine compound, where they function as protectors of
   the sacred precincts. In their role as guardians of the shrine they
   can be compared with the Niō, or "Benevolent Kings," *(No. 39)* who,
   with their powerful physiques and fearful countenances, perform
   a similar function for Buddhist temples.
      Usually one Koma-inu of a pair is portrayed with an open
   mouth and the other with its mouth closed, features associated with
   the first and last letters of the Sanskrit alphabet, *a* and *um*, and
   implying manifest power and latent might respectively. Here,
   however, both animals have their mouths open and their teeth
   bared. Splendid creatures, surging with vitality, they seem barely
   able to restrain themselves from springing to the attack. They
   were once covered with gold, but much of the pigment has since
   worn away, revealing the full strength and beauty of the carved
   wood beneath.

**53. FOX MESSENGERS OF THE GOD INARI,
PROTECTOR OF THE RICE CROP**
Muromachi Period, 15th-16th century
Height: 31 cm.
William Watson, London, England

Inari is the Shintō God or Goddess of Rice. His principal shrine,
and the prototype of others scattered throughout Japan, is just
south of Kyoto, near Fushimi, and is said to have been founded
in 711 A.D. Foxes are invariably associated with this god, either as
attributes or guardians, though the reasons for this association,
which is an ancient one, are difficult to determine. Frequently the
fox is referred to as the god's messenger. Today, pairs of foxes,
usually of stone, are often seen flanking the entrances to Inari
shrines. Used thus, their relationship with *koma-inu* is obvious.
Though this particular pair of foxes may look less like *koma-inu*,
it is extremely likely that they too were shrine guardians. Here,
also, the mouth of one is open, the mouth of the other closed;
and the very fact that they *are* a pair suggests the parallel.
Allowances must be made for the fact that *koma-inu* are mythical
animals of Chinese origin while here the sculptor was able to
rely on actual observation. These foxes seem wonderfully natural
with none of the stylized mock ferocity of the *koma-inu*. Yet they
are not without stylization of their own. Certain details, such
as the bellies and haunches, seem remarkably true to life, but
others—the muzzle of the fox at the left, for example—are
boldly simplified.

Both foxes show traces of brown pigment, possibly lacquer,
which seems to have covered much of the surface over a priming
of *gofun* or gesso. The hind legs of both animals are missing in part,
and an entire foreleg is missing from the fox at right. Parts of the
ears and paws of the fox at left have been restored.

The use of masks has a long history in Japan, extending back at least as far as the early seventh century, when the form of dance-drama known as *gigaku* was first introduced from the continent. *Gigaku* is thought to have been a kind of humorous interlude performed in connection with Buddhist rituals, probably as a form of comic relief from more solemn observances. *Bugaku* was a later, but related, form of dance-drama, associated chiefly with the Imperial Court.

The earliest type of mask represented here, however, the gyōdō mask *(No. 54)*, is more purely religious in nature. Gyōdō masks were developed during the Heian Period for use in solemn processions, usually in connection with the cult of Amida. Representing celestial beings such as bodhisattvas and apsaras, they are clearly related to the sculptural depictions of these same beings.

The Heian Period also saw the first appearance of a more popular form of entertainment using masks, *sarugaku*, or "monkey music." *Sarugaku* combined acrobatics, magic, and mime in witty, often satirical performances staged in conjunction with temple and shrine festivals. As unlikely as it might seem, *sarugaku* was the direct forerunner of Japan's loftiest form of dramatic expression, nō (often written noh), which was perfected during the late fourteenth and early fifteenth centuries by the actor Zeami (1363-1443).

Nō is drama raised to the level of ritual. Performed with a minimum of props against a stark setting, its unearthly, high-pitched music, slow, measured movements and gorgeous costumes create an unforgettable impression. The repertory is limited; the themes, drawn from history and legend, are almost invariably tragic, imbued with the Buddhist sense of the transitory nature of all things. The religious component was strong.

In nō, as in other forms of traditional Japanese theater, all roles, male or female, are played by men. The masks, carved from well-seasoned cypress or paulownia wood, are smaller and more light-weight than other Japanese masks and cover less of the face. Many of the masks are so subtle and ambiguous in expression that, manipulated by accomplished actors, they seem capable of convey-ing a whole range of conflicting emotions *(No. 56)*. Others, more obvious and fixed in expression, are more limited in the roles in which they can be used.

The perfection of the nō mask, with its extraordinary subtlety and expressiveness, depended upon certain prior technical develop-ments that had taken place in sculpture and the art of woodcarving in general. In full-fledged *yosegi* sculpture, the face is no longer part of the same block or post of wood as the head; it is a separate, shallow piece of wood that can be held and worked in the hand; in effect, a mask. The *yosegi* technique had already been perfected for well over a century by the time the first nō masks were carved. The carver was thus able to draw upon the technical experience of several generations of sculptors as well as the lengthy tradition of Japanese mask making.

54. GYŌDŌ MASK

Heian Period, dated 1158
Height: 21.6 cm.
Seattle Art Museum. Eugene Fuller Memorial Collection

Gyōdō is the term for a Buddhist ritual in which monks, clad in gorgeous robes and wearing masks, walk in procession around the temple precincts and past the principal icons. Such rituals are still performed today.

This mask, which represents a bodhisattva, was used in a procession enacting the *raigō*, the glorious vision greeting those who were welcomed into the Pure Land Paradise by Amida (Amitabha) and his attendants.

Judging from the relatively large number of such masks found in Western collections, these processions must have been staged with great frequency during the Heian Period, when the Amida cult was at the height of its popularity.

An inscription on the back of this mask gives a date corresponding to 1158 A.D. An incomplete set of gyōdō masks in the Tōdai-ji in Nara has been dated to the same year, raising the possibility that this mask once belonged to that set.

The two holes drilled at the top were presumably for the attachment of a metal crown of the sort still found in many of these masks. The crown would have fit against the recessed band above the ridge of hair, making the flatness of the top less obvious. The face is unusually broad, its expression one of great calmness and repose. Much of the gesso and polychrome has peeled off, but touches of color still remain, particularly on the hair and lips. Traces of a painted curl can still be made out on the forehead.

55. TSUINA MASK
Kamakura Period, 13th century
Height: 26.3 cm.
Kimbell Art Museum, Fort Worth

The Japanese scholar Shōichi Uehara thinks that this may well
be one of the oldest *tsuina* masks in existence. Carved for use in
the annual goblin-expelling ceremony held on the last day of winter,
such masks incurred rough usage and tended to be discarded and
replaced rather than treasured as keepsakes. For some reason,
this mask was an exception and was preserved for centuries in
the storehouses of the famous temple complex of Hōryū-ji near Nara.

The *tsuina* ceremony, which is still performed in some parts
of Japan, involves the ritual exorcism of the accumulated ills of the
past year. The highpoint of the ceremony is the simulated punish-
ment and expulsion of a man wearing a goblin mask. Most *tsuina*
masks differ from this one in having horns and being altogether
more fanciful and grotesque. The relative realism of this mask is one
feature supporting its attribution to the Kamakura Period. The
other is its extraordinary thinness.

The mask has an expression of intense ferocity. The brows are
pulled down steeply over the bulging, staring eyes, and the mouth,
squared off at the corner in a fiendish grimace, is open, exposing
sharp fangs.

The entire mask was covered with black lacquer then coated
with white clay over which colors were added: verdigris for the
skin, pink for the gums and linings of the eyes, and gold for
the teeth and bulging eyeballs. Moustache and beard hairs were
once set into holes still visible above the mouth and on the
jutting chin.

56. WAKA-ONNA: NŌ MASK
Muromachi Period (1392-1568)
Height: 17.7 cm.
The Cleveland Museum of Art. Purchase, John L. Severance Fund

There is something strangely haunting about this enigmatic mask
with its high forehead, narrow, wide-set eyes and full, slightly
parted lips. The eyes are turned down and crinkled at the corners;
the parted lips reveal a row of blackened teeth. The face is
unusually long and thin; otherwise it corresponds almost exactly
with the classic *waka-onna*, "young woman" type, which was
used in a great variety of women's roles. The subtle carving and
deliberate ambiguity of expression encourage the viewer to "read"
emotions into the mask, a quality that the knowing actor,
particularly one conscious of the varying effects produced by the
play of light and shade over its surface, could exploit to advantage.

   Much of the polychrome has chipped or flaked away. Painted
hair is still visible at the top of the mask, but there is no sign
of the artificial, "smudged" eyebrows that once would have
appeared high up on the forehead.

57. KO-BESHIMI: NŌ MASK

Muromachi Period (1392-1568)
Height: 20.3 cm.
The Cleveland Museum of Art. Purchase, John L. Severance Fund

This *ko-beshimi*, "small" or "lesser demon" mask, reflects an aspect of nō that seems to have less to do with the refined esthetic theories of Zeami and his followers than with popular demonology and rituals of exorcism. The relationship with the *tsuina* mask *(No. 55)* is obvious, especially in the turned down brows, bulging eyes and flaring nostrils. The face is squarer, however, and the mouth is tightly pursed, resulting in an expression which, though baleful, is decidedly less demonic. Sherman Lee points to the relationship between masks of the *beshimi* type and the faces of Buddhist guardian figures such as the Niō. Without question, there is a certain resemblance between this mask and the head of the closed-mouth Niō, Naraen Kongō *(No. 39)*, in this exhibition.

The eyes of the *tsuina* mask were covered with gilt; these are covered with metal and must have glinted strangely as they caught the light during a performance. Metal eyes of this sort were often used in masks representing supernatural beings.

The top of the mask is flattened off and outlined in black. This part of the mask would undoubtedly have been covered with a wig.

The most noticeable change to occur in Japanese sculpture after the Kamakura Period was a shift away from the dominance of Buddhism. Though icons continued to be made in great numbers, they tended to be made according to traditional formulas; there were few new developments. There were several reasons for this. One was that the periodic introduction of new forms of Buddhism from the continent, which had been such an important factor in Japanese religious life earlier, had all but ceased after the arrival of Zen in the thirteenth century. Zen itself, which had a strong iconoclastic bias, had little impact on sculpture other than in the field of portraiture. Sculpture was also affected by the shift of patronage away from the temples to secular centers of power, the courts of the *daimyō* (regional lords) and the shōgun. This marked the beginning of a gradual secularization of Japanese culture which was accelerated during the Momoyama Period when Nobunaga effectively broke the back of the Buddhist establishment by slaughtering thousands of monks and systematically destroying their temples.

The Momoyama Period also saw the increased importance of sculpture as an integral part of architecture. The beam end carvings *(No. 60)* in this exhibition are only one example of the many forms of carved wood ornamentation that gained currency at this time. Relief panels, carved openwork louvers *(ramma)*, and elaborate interbeam supports *(No. 63)* were others. Almost all of these were painted. The extravagance and assertiveness of the Momoyama Period is well symbolized by its architecture.

During the Edo Period, which followed, the progressive secularization of Japanese society continued. Population grew, and the merchant classes prospered, though held in check by an increasingly repressive government which seemed unable to cope with the complexities of the new money-based economy. The merchant classes, excluded either purposely or by their own preference from participation in the traditional cultural pursuits, developed their own lively subculture. Much of the vitality of the art of the Edo Period derives from this source. *Haiku, kabuki, ukiyo-e* — all are products of this subculture, as are such sturdy, humorous carvings as the image of Ebisu *(No. 60)*, the "Beckoning Cat" *(No. 65)*, or the small frog *(No. 66)*. The subculture had its more elegant side, however, as can be seen in such objects as the lacquer writing box *(No. 68)*.

Certain carvings in the exhibition derive from yet another tradition and are the products of another segment of Edo Period society. These are folk arts in the truest sense of the word and reflect the ingenuity, sound craftmanship and traditional beliefs of the rural Japanese *(Nos. 67 and 70)*.

58. SHŌTOKU TAISHI

Nambokuchō Period, mid 14th century
Height: 52.7 cm.
Private collection, anonymous

As mentioned earlier, Shōtoku Taishi was the subject of numerous paintings and sculptures from the late Heian Period on. We have already seen one sculpture of him *(no. 41)* dating from the Kamakura Period, but this one seems to belong to another tradition altogether. Carved almost entirely from a single block of wood, it has some of the sturdy, straightforward quality of folk art. This is particularly apparent in the four-square stance and undisguised symmetry of the body. Yet it is a work of considerable sophistication, and the face, especially, is carved with great subtlety. The prince is shown as a handsome, boyish figure of indeterminate age, wearing a loose shirt and baggy trousers. His hair is arranged in the style usually found in images representing him at age sixteen, ministering to his father; but he normally wears a priest's robe in such images and holds a censer. It is impossible to tell whether this figure once held a censer or not.

59. MONKEY
Muromachi Period (1392-1568)
Height: 29.8 cm.
Mr. Langdon J. Plumer, Exeter, New Hampshire

Even in his present condition, missing two limbs, there is something
convincingly lifelike about this little monkey. Crouching on his
haunches but leaning forward, his left hand on his knee, he peers
inquisitively off to his right. There is no way of knowing how
such a figure would have been used, though monkeys do appear
occasionally as the servant messengers or attendants of various
Shintō deities.

The monkey is carved from a single piece of wood with a
rectangular recess neatly hollowed out behind. It is unclear
whether this recess was ever covered with a back.

60. KIBANA (PAIR OF BEAM END CARVINGS)
Late Momoyama or early Edo Period, early 17th century
Height: 29.8 cm.; 30.5 cm.
Asian Art Museum of San Francisco, the Avery Brundage Collection

These dramatic carvings in the form of crouching lions were used
as ornamental beam ends, possibly in a gate. The fact that the
mouth of one lion is open and that of the other closed suggests an
analogy with *koma-inu (No. 52)* and *Niō (No. 39)* and further
supports the possibility that they were used in a gate or at least
somehow in connection with an entrance.

Carved with enormous energy and boldness, the animals themselves all but disappear in the flow of deeply carved, stylized swirls
representing the forehead hair and manes. Such energy is typical
of the Momoyama Period (1573-1615), the great age of castle
building, when the vigor and assertiveness of leaders like Nobunaga
and Hideyoshi galvanized Japanese society, giving new stimulus
and direction to the arts.

It is important to remember that these carvings were but one
element in a massive architectural ensemble, the basic intention
of which was to overawe and impress. During the Momoyama
Period, buildings became symbols of power, and sculpture became
the hand-maiden of architecture.

61. KANNON WITH BIRD HEADDRESS
By Enkū (1632-1695), *ca.* 1680s
Height: 52.1 cm.
Mrs. Usher Coolidge, Ipswich, Massachusetts

There is very little in the earlier Buddhist art of Japan to prepare
us for the sudden emergence, in the seventeenth century, of the
work of the priest-sculptor Enkū, whose rough-hewn, expressionistic images seem closer, at first glance, to the art of certain modern
European sculptors than to the products of traditional Buddhist
workshops. Enkū turned his back on the *yosegi* technique and all
the preliminary planning and painstaking joinery it implied,
favoring instead a more direct approach to a single block. In his
later work, especially, he virtually *attacks* the wood, creating
sharp, cliff-like projections and bold undercuts; and he makes no
attempt to disguise his toolmarks but actually exploits them (as
here, in the strange bird-like headdress) for expressionistic or
descriptive purposes.

Yet, for all his originality, Enkū did draw on earlier traditions.
His deliberate use of toolmarks may owe something to the
precedent of *natabori* sculpture, numerous examples of which
he must have seen during a three-year sojourn in Northern Japan
and Hokkaidō early in his career. Even a feature as distinctive
as the several saw-tooth projections on either side of this figure
almost certainly reflect Enkū's familiarity with the seventh century
Wei Dynasty-inspired sculpture at Hōryū-ji, where he spent the
year 1671 pursuing his studies of Buddhism.

Enkū seems to have preferred remote, mountainous districts and
must have spent much of his life actively engaged in missionary
work in such areas. He undoubtedly saw his sculpture as an integral
part of his religious vocation and is said to have made a vow to
carve 120,000 images during his lifetime. Such a vow reflected
the widespread Mahāyāna belief that the merit accumulated
through the repetition of a pious act would eventually benefit all
sentient beings *(cf. Nos. 34 and 35)*. Clearly much in Enkū's method
of working—his preference for images of relatively small size and
his summary treatment of details—must have been dictated by
a genuine desire to fulfill his vow.

There is still much that is unknown about this fascinating artist.
It is known that he was associated, early in his career, with
Shugendō Buddhism, an ascetic cult active in mountainous areas.
He also carved Shintō images. Such contacts almost certainly
account for some of the obvious syncretic elements in Enkū's work.

62. EBISU (ONE OF THE SEVEN GODS OF GOOD FORTUNE)

Edo Period, 17th-18th century
Height: 84.7 cm.
William Rockhill Nelson Gallery of Art-Atkins Museum
of Fine Arts, Kansas City, Missouri. Nelson Fund

It is hard to think of this figure as anything other than a jovial
sprite; yet he represents Ebisu, one of the *shichi-fuku-jin*, "seven
gods of good luck." He was particularly popular during the
Edo Period when, as the God of Food and Patron of
Fishermen, he was enshrined in virtually every household in
Japan. Yet he was probably never thought of as a deity in the
strictest sense of that word; certainly he was too humble and
domestic to be the object of any special veneration, in spite of
the fact that several popular festivals and observances centered
about him, especially in the larger cities. In general he was
probably treated as nothing more than a mascot or simple emblem
of good luck.

This is an unusually large image of Ebisu, and must have been
intended for some fairly public setting, perhaps a popular shop
or the meeting rooms of an inn. The simulated rock pedestal is also
unusual, though similar pedestals are quite common in Buddhist
iconography. Here it may simply represent a rocky bank and
refer to the god's role as the patron of fishermen. The bamboo
fishing pole and the *tai*, or sea bream (itself a symbol of good
fortune), are his chief attributes, though he is also almost always
shown, as here, in court costume wearing an official cap or *kammuri*.

The *shichi-fuku-jin* are a relatively late grouping of divinities
of various origins: Buddhist, Taoist, and Shintō. There is no
evidence of their existence as a group before the seventeenth century.
The other six gods are: Fukurokujū, the god of longevity; Daikoku,
the god of wealth; Hotei *(see No. 19)*, the god of contentment;
Bishamon, originally one of the Guardian Kings of Buddhism;
Benten, the goddess of love and music; and Jurōjin, the god of
scholarly success.

124

63. KAERUMATA (WIND AND THUNDER GODS)
Early Edo Period, 17th century
Height: 99.1 cm.
Asian Art Museum of San Francisco, the Avery Brundage Collection

These arch-shaped relief carvings were made as beam supports,
the beams fitting into the shallow notches at the top of each arch.
The Japanese word for these supports, *kaerumata*, means "frog's
legs," which they are apparently thought to resemble.

The two ogre-like creatures are the Wind God, with his bag of
wind thrown over his shoulder, and the Thunder God, surrounded
by his thunder drums and clutching a drumstick in each hand.
The two figures resemble one another closely in build, in garb, and
in general attitude. Both have broad noses, bristling beards, and
shaggy hair; both are shown running in a similar fashion across
stylized clouds. The Wind God, however, differs from the Thunder
God in having two stubby horns. The carving in both pieces is
vigorous but relatively crude.

The Wind and Thunder Gods were popular subjects during the
Edo Period and were a frequently used motif in architecture,
especially at roof ends, where they were used as charms to protect
the building against damage from storms.

64. SAKE SIGN
Edo Period, 18th-19th century
Height: 90.2 cm.
Seattle Art Museum. Eugene Fuller Memorial Collection

Carved signboards flourished during the Edo Period. This one, evidently made for a sake shop, is in the form of a traditional sake barrel wrapped in matting and tied with stout rope. Though actually quite flat, it very successfully conveys a sense of the barrel's volume. The humorous depiction of the huge, child-like *sumō* wrestler is carved with controlled chisel marks that imitate the bold but mannered brushstrokes found in *ema* (Shintō votive paintings) or kabuki posters of the late eighteenth century. Though not an example of "fine" art, this signboard is no mere journeyman's work either; it has all the earmarks of a still very vigorous tradition.

65. CAT
Edo Period (1615-1867)
Height: 31.7 cm.
Mr. and Mrs. James W. Alsdorf, Winnetka, Illinois

Even today, *maneki-neko*, "beckoning cats," are often seen in shop windows or restaurant entrances in Japan, where they are used as talismans or mascots to attract clientele. It is not known when such figures were first used for this purpose, though it is known that they were popular already in the late Edo Period. Present-day *maneki-neko* are usually made of clay, but in other respects they closely resemble this piece, even in such details as the collar with its suspended bell. The cat is always shown, as here, sitting on its haunches with one paw upraised attracting the attention of passers-by. It should be noted, by the way, that the Japanese beckon people by waving to them with their hands *palm outward*.

66. FROG
Edo Period (1615-1867)
Height: 5.7 cm.
Mr. and Mrs. James W. Alsdorf, Winnetka, Illinois

Unlike the other Japanese objects that have been discussed so far,
all of which originally had some specific use, as icons, items of
ritual paraphernalia, or architectural elements, for example, this
frog—or is it a toad?—seems to have been made with no particular
function in mind. The Japanese have always been keenly observant
of animal life, and their poetry is full of references to insects,
birds, and other creatures, including such garden varieties as toads
and frogs. Here the anonymous carver has clearly taken great
delight in his subject, contrasting the smooth underbelly with the
warty back and making the most of the wide mouth and bulging
eyes. The rough texture of the back is ingeniously rendered
in the simplest way possible, by making systematic use of the chisel-
marks themselves.

67. CARP (JIZAI-KAGI)
   Edo Period (1615-1867)
   Length: 48.2 cm.
   Seattle Art Museum. Eugene Fuller Memorial Collection

Sensitively carved from hard wood—possibly *keyaki*, or zelkova—
this carp *jizai-kagi* shows none of the extreme stylization found
in some forms of Japanese folk art and also lacks the rough-hewn
appearance of other folk objects. Yet it *was* made for use in a farm
house, as a device for regulating the height of iron vessels
(especially tea kettles) suspended over an open fire pit, and
shows the wear and polish that one would expect from an object
that has had generations of handling. Such *jizai-kagi*, "free-hanging
hooks", were generally carved in the shape of something associated
with water—an aquatic plant or a fish, for instance—or something
of auspicious import, such as a mallet or a fan. The carp manages
to qualify in both categories. As a symbol of fortitude and
perseverance, it was associated with sons and promising young
manhood. Carp banners—one for each son—are still flown at
households all over Japan on Boys' Day.

68. SCHOLAR'S WRITING BOX
Late Edo Period, 19th century
Length: 24 cm.
Art Institute of Chicago. Gift of the Woman's Board and
the Community Associates of the Art Institute of Chicago

In sheer decorative flair, this handsome nineteenth century writing box can easily hold its own with the finest lacquer work of earlier periods. The cover has been deliberately carved to resemble rough, weathered wood, which serves as a dramatic foil for the dark red lobsters. The lobsters are of lacquer, modelled in relief, and are rendered in naturalistic detail with spiny backs and long trailing antennae. The inside of the box is of lustrous, dark lacquer with flecks of sprinkled gold. The bold contrast of the rugged cover with the understated elegance of the interior seems typically Japanese,

Yet—also typically Japanese—the box is eminently functional for all its stylishness. As has always been true with the best of Japanese decorative art, the box sustains a delicate balance between excess of artifice and unaffected simplicity.

Boxes of this same general type, known as *suzuribako*—literally, "ink stone boxes"—have been made in Japan for centuries. The recessed well in the bottom is for the ink stone itself; the metal receptacle is for a water dropper. The box would also have held brushes and paper.

132

69. GURI LACQUER BOX
Late Edo Period, *ca.* 1800
Height: 3.8 cm.
Diameter: 10.8 cm.
Seattle Art Museum. Eugene Fuller Memorial Collection

Though there is wood at the core of this little box, much of its actual thickness is the result of applying successive layers of colored lacquer over the wood. The scroll pattern on the cover is carved through as many as ten of these layers. The colors used are red, black, green, and yellow. The carving itself is executed with impressive authority.

The inspiration for carved lacquer boxes like this, using the so-called *guri* (curves and rings) pattern, is ultimately Chinese. *No. 69* is more typically Japanese in taste. The Chinese inspiration of this piece is also attested to by the fanciful, contemporary "signature" on the bottom, ascribing it to the early Ming Chinese lacquer artist, Chang Ch'eng.

70. BIRD

Edo Period (1615-1867)
Height: 39 cm. (including base)
Mr. and Mrs. Myron S. Falk, Jr., New York City

Carvings similar to this, but smaller and more brightly painted, are still being made in Japan today. This earlier piece, however, has a sculptural quality and air of mystery about it that is unusual. Like many folk carvings of the Edo Period, particularly those from rural areas, it is darkened from the smoke of the open fire pits common in traditional farm houses. Traces of paint can still be made out under the soot on some of the tail feathers, however, and painted feet are shown projecting from the bird's body on top of the base.

Such carvings are a tribute to the native ingenuity of the rural Japanese craftsman. Everything is rendered in the simplest way possible, and only the most telling details are indicated, such as the wing and tail feathers, which have been created by making shallow slices into the wood and relying on its natural tendency to curl out. Chisel marks have been used to suggest the plumage of the body. The entire piece—bird and perch—has been carved from a single section of a tree trunk or limb, the basic shape and diameter of which is still preserved in the base.

PATRONS

This is the fifth and final exhibition in the Masterworks in Wood series, a Bicentennial program of the Portland Art Museum. The series has been supported by generous grants from the National Endowment for the Arts and the American Revolution Bicentennial Commission of Oregon, and by donations from individuals, corporations and private foundations, including the following:

Activities Council
Portland Art Association

Bank of California

Board of Trustees
Portland Art Association

Crown Zellerbach

Mr. and Mrs. Paul Feldenheimer

First National Bank of Oregon

Georgia-Pacific Foundation

Edmund Hayes

Carl and Alma Johnson Fund

Louisiana-Pacific Foundation

Mr. and Mrs. Frederick C. MacDonald

David Mason Trust

Pacific Northwest Bell

Pacific Power and Light

Pope & Talbot, Inc.

Mr. and Mrs. W. E. Roberts

Skyline Foundation, Inc.

U. S. National Bank of Oregon

Weyerhaeuser Company Foundation

Willamette Industries

Women's Council, Portland Art Association

Zellerbach Paper Company

Catalogue design:
Charles S. Politz
with the assistance of Jeff Dayne
and additional help of Robert Reynolds

Typography:
Schlegel Typesetting Co.

Lithography:
Durham & Downey, Inc.